Black Man Listen

The life of JR Ralph Casimir

Kathy Casimir MacLean

PAPILLOTE PRESS
London and Trafalgar, Dominica

For my sons
Calum, Ruairidh, Tormod and Fearchar
and for my grandchildren
Jacob and Freya

'Bringing the gifts that my ancestors gave
I am the dream and the hope of the slave'
MAYA ANGELOU

CONTENTS

*JR Ralph Casimir (1898-1996) in Dominica,
date unknown*

1

Memories
Near and Far

Joseph Raphael Ralph Casimir was my grandfather. He was a short, bespectacled black man (his height was recorded as 5ft 3ins in his passport). Small in stature he might have been but he made an important contribution to the political history of the Caribbean and the literature of Dominica, his birthplace.

I write this biography because it is about an ordinary man who built his life on principles which were shaped by his experiences, by his compassion, and by a desire to make life better for the ordinary people of Dominica. I intend to tell the story of Ralph Casimir's long life (1898-1996) not only by drawing on available historical evidence but from my own personal perspective and from the memories of those who knew him.

Casimir was a founding member of the Dominica Division of the Universal Negro Improvement Association (UNIA), spearheaded by Marcus Garvey in Harlem in 1917, and was the organiser and general secretary of the Dominican branch from 1919-23. He played a critical role in building the movement both in Dominica and in the Caribbean at a time when the Anglophone Caribbean was British and when the rights of its people were severely restricted. During his life, he was a bookbinder, commission agent, solicitor's clerk and cantor for the Roman Catholic Cathedral in the island's capital, Roseau. He served as a Roseau town councillor, and was secretary of several political organisations; most importantly, he was secretary to the famous and influential West Indian Conference held in Dominica in 1932 which, for the first time, addressed the political future of Britain's Caribbean colonies. He was also a poet, writing poetry over seven decades, and publishing nine books of poetry and Dominica's first poetry anthologies. Much of his poetry was influenced by his political beliefs.

My earliest memories of my grandfather are of his visits to our family home at King's Hill, on the outskirts of Roseau, in the 1950s and 1960s. Perched midway up the hill, the house, which was destroyed by the fury of Hurricane David[1] in 1979, was a sprawling bungalow with wide verandas at the front and back, surrounded by a garden of fruit trees.

Grandpa would arrive in the late afternoon while it was still light and the long shadows were beginning to fall. He often sat on the dark-green wooden bench, with a drink clinking with ice cubes, while I, with my siblings and cousins, played hopscotch or skipping games on the *glacee*,[2] opposite a broad-leaved mango tree. There, he would have long conversations with my maternal great-grandmother, Marie Lucie Olivaccé, sometimes known as Ma Percy,[3] as she sat in her cane rocking chair. Their voices were a background to our play.

When I was very young, Grandpa would put up with me bouncing on his knee and we would sing a nursery rhyme about galloping horses which would end with him pretending to drop me between his legs. I thought it was highly entertaining. As I grew older, he would more than likely find me immersed in a book. He would ruffle my hair and say, 'What are you reading, child? Hope it's teaching you something.' Or 'You should find a good light to read in. Careful you don't spoil your eyes.' As was customary, on his arrival we would all stop whatever we were doing to troop over and kiss him dutifully and wait to be dismissed before resuming our activity.

When my father, Rupert Casimir, came home from work, the two men would sit in the early evening as the sun set talking in

2

Casimir family album

King's Hill, the childhood home on the outskirts of Roseau of the author, Kathy Casimir MacLean.

comfortable voices about the happenings of the week. They talked of my grandfather's projects and interests and my father's plans for the future. My father would smoke his pipe, while my grandfather sat in the rocking chair now vacated by my great-grandmother, his hands clasped behind his head.

We always knew that Grandpa was about to arrive. We could hear his whistle as he approached. He made an art of whistling and it was my first introduction to classical music as he would whistle classical tunes; it was from him that I learned the names of Mozart and Chopin and then associated them with the records that my father played in his study. Grandpa always left us by eight o'clock. He would kiss us goodbye, don his hat and stride off into the darkness whistling his way down the hill towards the town.

When I was 12 years old, my father was appointed to a job at the United Nations Economic Commission for Africa as a statistician. A few days before our departure for Addis Ababa in November 1963, just as the sun was lowering in the west, preparing for its dramatic drop into the sea, Grandpa made the journey up the hill. As always, his approach was heralded by his whistling. He was carrying a large brown parcel.

We sat around, while he was being refreshed with a glass of lime squash, as he talked to us about our luck at moving to a country with great traditions. He spoke in admiring terms about Haile Selassie of Ethiopia: he was the Emperor, King of Kings, the Lion of Judah. His people had never been enslaved and they had defeated Mussolini and his Italian occupation. How lucky we would be to live in Africa, the birthplace of some of our ancestors. I got the feeling that Grandpa wished that he could accompany us on what he obviously viewed as a wonderful adventure. He spoke of the pride of the Ethiopian people who had not allowed the Italians to defeat them or break their spirit. It was an important conversation as before this I just knew that we were going to some place in Africa. Many of my contemporaries seemed to find this news a bit shocking as we were all very ignorant of life on that continent.

Years later, I discovered that my grandfather had been in regular correspondence[4] with the English suffragist Sylvia Pankhurst and a regular contributor to the *New Times and Ethiopia News*, the newspaper which she published and edited in London from 1936, after the Italian invasion of Ethiopia.

My grandfather's parcel contained a gift of a rather splendid children's encyclopaedia in 20 parts, as well as *The White Nile* and *The Blue Nile*, books by Alan Moorehead which were exciting and dramatic accounts of four explorations in Africa. The Blue Nile begins its journey to the Mediterranean at Lake Tana in Ethiopia and joins with the White Nile in Sudan. Having said his fond farewells and gained promises that we would write, he left us and as he whistled his way down the hill I wondered when I would next hear him whistle.

While we lived at King's Hill, in an extended family, with my maternal great-grandmother, an aunt, uncle, and cousins, my paternal grandparents lived in the centre of Roseau. When their house had been built towards the end of the 18th century, it looked onto cobbled

*Ralph Casimir on the veranda of his home
in Roseau, 1978*

streets and towards the broad Roseau River as it met the sea. Roseau
had once been the fertile fishing village of Sairi, inhabited by the
Kalinago people for hundreds of years before Columbus, before the
French and their slaves had settled it and eradicated the profusion of
troublesome reeds which had given the town its name.

My grandfather's house, at 60 Old Street, in which he and my
grandmother, Thelma, brought up their family of 15 children, was
built according to the French colonial style of its time. It was a large
wooden house fashioned from planks of local timber. The two wide-
set doors at the front of the ground floor opened into a small courtyard
which shielded the house from the road. The first set of doors led to
the drawing room with its highly polished wooden floors scattered
with patterned rugs, a caned mahogany chaise longue, its thin flock
mattress covered in a heavy patterned fabric. There were cushioned,
dark wooden armchairs and two side tables where, among the
photographs, the long-necked porcelain and glass oil lamps were

placed. These were used whenever there were the fairly frequent power cuts. In the corner was a glass cabinet which held precious china and a variety of ornaments.

The second set of external doors opened into the room which had become my grandfather's study. This room was lined with books and filing cabinets. Some of the books he had bound himself, including his compilation of Negro poetry.[5] On the walls were pictures of Grandpa's icons, among them Booker T Washington, Marcus Garvey and Haile Selassie. The desk was a wooden bureau with brass handles and locks. This was where he wrote his letters, articles and poetry; where he read, studied and worked. Many years later in 1984, he placed the Golden Drum, the highest national award for culture for his contribution to the island's literature, on the shelf behind his desk.

Children were not allowed into the study except to be formally greeted and questioned about school and reading activities but I later knew that it was also in to this room that my father, the boy Rupert, had sneaked in 1939. He was in trouble with a local vendor who had allowed him to mount up a debt for buljaw[6] sandwiches, and it was there that he had knelt and prayed for help. Guided by a mysterious beam of light he had located the key to the desk drawer which held the desperately needed two shillings. He took the coins and paid off his debt. This act, which resulted in a severe punishment, taught him never again to spend money that he didn't already possess.

Beyond these two rooms was the dining room with large open windows looking out into the back garden. As is typical of this type of architecture, the stairs leading to the elaborately carved overhanging front veranda are set outside the house. Access to the upper rooms is through the French doors which open onto the veranda, while a set of external stairs leads to the rooms on the next floor. Another set of stairs led up to the two rooms in the garret. The partition walls in the jumble of rooms were topped with a fretwork partition bringing light and air.

In the back yard was the traditional outside kitchen, built as a separate stone construction, with its stone oven and range. By the 1950s, it had been wired for gas and electricity and also housed a modern oven and fridge; the inner room, used as a store, would have once been the maid's bedroom.

My oldest aunt, Octavia, used to have her sewing machine in the front bedroom where she also slept; she sewed dresses with tiny waists and full skirts for herself and her sisters. My grandparents' bedroom was next door and it was in that room that in 1996 I attended the nine nights of prayer for the safe passing over of my grandfather's soul. By then my grandmother had been dead for almost ten years.

When I visited with my own family in 1978, the house and its furniture seemed unchanged: the same light-coloured walls, the same old, highly polished furniture and my grandmother still stubbornly maintaining her outside kitchen. The aunts, who had lived there in my childhood, were all abroad and there was no one to shatter the tranquility of the day. My grandfather dandled my two-year-old on his knee whistling tunefully just as he had to me when I was a little girl.

Harry Sealey, a Trinidadian living in Dominica, who became one of my grandfather's acolytes in his last years, tells the story of helping him paint the house in the 'liberation colours'. (This is reported in greater detail in chapter 7.) Sadly the house no longer exists, it was sold after my grandfather's death and eventually demolished; where it once stood there is an open wound.

I believe that I was in my late twenties before I became aware of my grandfather's political history. I was a child of the 1950s and I was born into a colonial society in which our education was strictly colonial. We were not taught our own history but that of Britain and the empire. Any reference to historical fact was cloaked in mythology so, for

Ralph Casimir, aged 91, in 1989. 'I was a bit of a firebrand when I was young.'

example, Jacko and Mabouya, famed maroon chiefs, were the bogeymen of my childhood occupying equal status with the soucouyant and ladjablès.[7]

Dominica's connections with the UNIA remained unknown to Dominicans until students began to attend the University of the West Indies where a course in West Indian history became a compulsory module in the 1960s for all first-year undergraduate students across all UWI campuses.[8] For me, however, it was when my husband, on our first visit together to Dominica, asked Grandpa about his life as a young man that I heard for the first time of his connection with Marcus Garvey, the UNIA and his correspondence with many icons of black history and Sylvia Pankhurst.

The last visit that I had with my grandfather was in the summer of 1989. Every day he would be brought to my parents' home for lunch. He loved a rum punch as a pre-lunch drink. Afterwards, we would sit on the front porch and chat. It was then that I discovered that he had bequeathed his UNIA-related documents to the Schomburg Center for Research in Black Culture in Harlem, New York City. He reminisced about his relationship with Edward Scobie, the Dominican-born journalist and publisher known for his early research

8

on black British history; lamented the passing of his friends, in particular, the doyen of the Harlem Renaissance Langston Hughes, and Elias Nassief of Dominica. He shared with me the poems he had written to commemorate the deaths of my grandmother and Nassief. He was relaxed and joyful. We took many excursions together to restaurants and the beach. And on each occasion he would carry his latest poetry pamphlet to distribute to whoever he met. He loved the visits to the seaside and would roll around in the water like a contented porpoise. My children found him intriguing, and that autumn my 11-year-old son wrote a school essay about his great-grandfather entitled, 'The most interesting person I have met'. Grandpa died on 8 March 1996 aged 97.

2
The Road
to Roseau

The village of St Joseph, where Ralph Casimir was born on 24 September 1898, lies halfway up the west coast of Dominica set in a valley between the towering mountain of Morne Diablotin and the more modest Morne Couronne. Typically for rural villages of the time, the majority of its inhabitants were fishermen and peasant farmers, whose land provided them with most of their food. They may also have grown cocoa and limes as cash crops. Nearby was the Hillsborough estate, modest in Caribbean terms but sizeable for Dominica with one of the largest water mills on the island.[9] It is likely that Casimir was a descendant of one of the estate's slave families, emancipated in 1834.

Casimir's parents, Dudley, a carpenter, and Maria (née Toulon), a seamstress, were not part of the middle class but were none the less aspirational. They were well regarded and well known in the area. They would have lived in a traditional two or three-roomed wooden house with a half-hip galvanised roof overhanging the veranda. Known in Kwéyòl as a *ti kai*, it would have been raised from the ground on stilts. Dudley Casimir, who was a fine carpenter with a good reputation, would have worked on it, building extra rooms as needed. The kitchen was an out-building where food would be prepared and cooked using a coal pot and an open fire. Their toilet requirements would have been met by a pit latrine.

Postcard of St Joseph, the village on Dominica's west coast where Casimir was born and raised.

St Joseph was a cluster of similar wooden houses. The roads between them were stony, dirt tracks worn down by the constant tread of feet. The tufts of grass which sprung up alongside provided grazing for the resident goats tethered next to the houses. The church was already the iconic landmark that it is today. Its cruciform stone building had replaced the existing 1740 church in 1846 but it was not until 1891 that the front facade was completed.

In the same year that Casimir was born, the British tightened their hold on Dominica by introducing the Crown Colony Bill, by which the few enfranchised citizens of the British colony of Dominica lost the right to vote for elected representatives. As a consequence, many Dominicans resigned from every government board in protest and vowed that they would not serve again until their rights were regained. ARC Lockhart, a prominent newspaper owner, politician and distant relative of the author Jean Rhys, was one who was vociferous in his opposition, and he gave up his honorary position as justice of the peace and repeatedly refused a Legislative Council seat. Despite these difficulties, the new administration operated smoothly. It was no doubt aided by the arrival of a new administrator, Hesketh Bell, in 1899, which, according to Dominican historian Joseph A Boromé, 'signalled the beginning of the most brilliant administration the island ever experienced'.[10]

Dominica was never an important British colony. This was in part due to its mountainous terrain and dense rainforest and its mainly absentee British landowners. Its main value to Britain had been strategic. The British historian JA Froude, who visited the island in 1887, said that he was ashamed to see the British flag flying in Dominica as Britain had done 'nothing, absolutely nothing, to introduce her own civilisation, and thus Dominica is English only in name'.[11]

Descriptions of Roseau, the capital, some 12 miles south of St Joseph, were of a dilapidated town with neglected buildings and cobbled streets last laid by the French in the early 18th century and now beset with weeds between the cobbles. Hesketh Bell reported that

A street in Roseau, the capital of Dominica, at the turn of the 20th century.

all the public buildings were in a wretched state, devoid of paint; the usual source of lighting being a few kerosene lamps. There were only three carriages on the whole island and only a few miles of drivable road. 'Most of the island,' he reported, 'is still under virgin forest.'[12] By the late 19th century, the population was around 28,000, most of whom were Roman Catholic and lived mainly in coastal villages, such as St Joseph.

During Casimir's youth in St Joseph, conditions would have been even more stringent than those in the capital. Communication with Roseau and the other villages strung along the coast was on foot, by horse or donkey or, for those rich enough, there was the weekly boat from Roseau.

When reflecting on villages such as St Joseph, it is useful to remember the roots of such communities and the influences which dictated the ethnic composition, language and culture of its people.

The history of Dominica is a complex one. Its first inhabitants we have knowledge of migrated to Dominica from the banks of the Orinoco River in South America more than 3,000 years ago. Information about the different groups and waves of migration has been pieced together through archeological study. It was the Kalinago who named the island Waitukubuli (Tall is her body). They were the inhabitants who met and traded with the first Europeans. The island was sighted by Christopher Columbus on his second voyage, on 3 November 1493, and named Dominica as it was a Sunday. When the Spanish finally found a suitable harbour, they were impressed by the beauty of the island. Lennox Honychurch reports that Nicolo Syllacio, a translator of accounts of the voyage, recorded: 'Dominica is remarkable for the beauty of its mountains and the amenity of its verdue and must be seen to be believed.'[13]

The Spanish never settled the island but in order to replenish the slave labour in their other colonies they are reputed to have captured and enslaved Kalinagos, renamed Caribs by the Spanish, from a number of Leeward islands including Dominica. Spanish missionaries were brought to the island and met with hostility. For many years from around 1535, the island served as an outpost for supplying ships sailing to and from the Americas with wood and water.

Dominica remained unclaimed by European powers until it was settled by French planters in 1635. England, France's rival, soon vied for control. In 1686 both nations agreed to relinquish the island to the Kalinagos, yet repeatedly returned. By 1750, the Kalinagos had retreated to the rugged windward coast. Then in 1763, France ceded Dominica to England in the Treaty of Paris. It was during this period that John Greg, a businessman from Belfast, purchased the land at the mouth of the Layou valley in 1765, which would become Hillsborough estate. The French captured the island in 1778, but the English regained control in 1783.

Enslaved Africans were brought to the island as a result of European settlement to provide labour to work the estates. Links with the French islands continued; and runaway slaves from the French islands and displaced mulattos sought refuge in Dominica.[14] This legacy of French occupation and migration meant that the people remained more French than British. Even today, many families still have relations, as well as both linguistic and cultural ties, in the French Antilles.

The Casimir family of St Joseph would have spoken both the French-based Kwéyòl and English. For many Dominicans, Kwéyòl was their mother tongue. As Governor Bell had put it: 'The great majority of coloured people speak nothing but patois.'[15] At that time, Kwéyòl was known as patois and often described as 'broken French'. The French Creole language had developed during slavery and is also spoken in Haiti, Guadeloupe, Martinique and St Lucia. Its vocabulary is derived mainly from French with some words from the Niger Congo languages and the languages of the indigenous population: '... in an analysis of the Creole languages of the Caribbean as well as Caribbean culture, it is clear that Europe has affected Africa but equally Africa has affected Europe: the words are European, but the syntax is African.'[16]

English, however, was the official language in Dominica, and children who had access to education would have had to speak English at school. For people such as Dudley and Maria, who felt it important that their children should be able to rise out of their situation, education and the gathering of knowledge provided the route. Knowledge existed in books and in the newspapers which arrived by steamship from Roseau.

The Lady Mico Charity, set up to provide education for the formerly enslaved, had established 20 elementary schools in Dominica by 1840 — their non-denominational teaching was welcomed by the British government. Then, in 1853, an Education Act to operate secular schools was passed. However, the scheme met with opposition, and it was realised that the inclusion of the Catholic Church in the setting up of schools would be beneficial. The lieutenant governor noted that 'to do anything that would in any way withdraw children from the parental control of the priest' would be a mistake. In 1867, a new Education Bill was passed to bring about cooperation between the Board of Education and the Catholic Church. The result was a rapid increase in the number of Catholic elementary schools across the island, including the one in St Joseph.[17]

The three Casimir children, Ralph, his younger brother, Hubert, and Meredith, his younger sister, were among those who were able to go to school. Not everyone attended school on a regular basis as parents would withdraw their children to work in their 'gardens'. St Joseph's Elementary School was a wooden building with one long room in which the older and younger children would have been separated by a blackboard. The main writing implements were a slate and a slate

*Casimir (top left), with his mother (seated) and
younger brother Hubert and sister Meredith.
Date unknown.*

marker. Some of the older children may have had some access to
precious exercise books in which they could write their compositions
and copy information from the blackboard. Learning would have been
principally by rote and chanting. The standards in schools were low,
and pupils were unlikely to be taught by qualified practitioners.

Outside the schoolroom, music was an important part of family life
for the Casimirs. Dudley had acquired a violin which he played with
accomplishment, well enough to play in church. Maria and
subsequently their children sang in the church choir. This was a
practice which Casimir maintained throughout his life. He was a
cantor in Roseau Cathedral (I was often aware that he was singing in
the choir stalls overhead whenever I attended a high Mass). The
family's faith formed the centre of their lives. It was a faith that

remained important to Ralph Casimir. They were a close family and would have spent the evenings at home in the dim glow of the oil-filled lamps.

Many years later my grandfather continued to instil this practice in the family by insisting that everyone had to be gathered indoors by 8.00pm, with doors locked and lights extinguished by nine o'clock. My father Rupert often told us the story of his own conflict with his father over this rule. One evening he was out attending rehearsals for *The Gondoliers*,[18] and returned home after nine only to find the house in darkness and the doors barred. No amount of knocking and calling would secure admittance. He was able to gain entry to the Union Club and spent the night there.[19] The next day my stubborn grandfather showed no remorse and was unbending about the rule. It was then that my 21-year-old father left home to lodge with his mother's cousin, his godfather Evarard Giraud.

As a boy growing up in St Joseph, Casimir would have been expected to make a contribution to household chores, to weed the back yard with a cutlass and to accompany his father when planting or harvesting ground provisions (yam, dasheen, sweet potatoes) and bananas. His leisure time would have been spent with other youths — picking mangoes, guavas, oranges, kenips or occasionally raiding other people's fruit trees. They would chase birds and hunt them with a homemade catapult or search for large land crabs. He would have been with the boys jumping off the jetty into the sea and swimming back to the shore. Climbing trees and playing cricket with a homemade bat on any suitable patch of flat ground was another pastime.

Ralph Casimir's education at St Joseph's Elementary School from 1903 to 1914 was very basic but ignited in him a desire for knowledge and to expand his own learning. He had a keen interest in the world around him. This is reflected in the careful drawings that he executed,

Casimir, aged 13, captioned in his own handwriting.

documented in papers which survive from his years as a pupil teacher. Many of these drawings point to a particular interest in biology and botany. Among his papers are drawings of warships and buildings, some no doubt copied from books but some, such as his local church and the Roseau Cathedral, were from observation.

At that time, as the son of a carpenter and seamstress in St Joseph, further or higher education would have been beyond his wildest dreams. He must have had aspirations to be an artist as he was accepted on a drawing correspondence course in 1918 by the A.B.C. School of Drawing at The Strand in London, but had to give it up as he could not afford the fees. An accompanying letter, dated 17 May 1918, states, 'Your copying of a hand shows great promise, you have a good idea of form and proportion... you have a talent which only needs development by the right sort of tuition.'[20]

In 1914, the year he left school at the age of 16, Casimir returned to his old school as a pupil teacher. This apprenticeship was awarded to a student who showed dedication, scholarship and promise. His job would have been to support the teacher and give instruction to the younger pupils. He was employed in this position for two years. With what little money he earned, he bought and subscribed to newspapers, magazines and journals. In St Joseph, he would have had access to the *Dominica Guardian* and out-of-date copies of magazines such as the *National Geographic*. By visiting Roseau he would have been able to acquire second-hand reading material.

At some point during Casimir's childhood Maria had become estranged from Dudley and moved to Roseau with Meredith. There is no record of what prompted the rift or indeed this move from St Joseph. I can only speculate that Maria believed that there would be greater opportunities for them in Roseau, more so than employment as a labourer at Hillsborough estate which by that time had become a

The Roseau library, opened in 1906, where Casimir did much of his early reading.

successful producer of limes. As a seamstress in Roseau, she would also have access to a greater number of clients.

In 1916, and now aged 18, Casimir joined his mother in Roseau. He felt he could no longer remain at the school as he had had a disagreement with the headmaster and also felt the need to expand his horizons. Then, at the end of August 1916, a devastating hurricane, in which 50 people died, swept the island with crops and homes destroyed. A report from the colonial engineer to the administrator, stated that 'all the rivers came down with extreme violence... The Macoucherie River [near St Joseph] rising from the same hills as the Layou... brought the debris from practically unknown regions.'[21] This event may have also contributed to Casimir's decision to leave St Joseph for Roseau. There, the young Casimir became a regular user of the new and nominally free Carnegie library, opened in 1906. Although the inscription on the building described itself as such, it was only the use of the Reading Room that was in fact 'free'. Only subscribers had borrowing privileges. It was not until 1945, when a British Council project, designed to set up regional libraries in the Caribbean supplying books free of charge, that borrowing became free for all Dominicans.[22]

Once resident in Roseau, Casimir was prepared to do almost anything that enabled him to work with the printed word. He soon found employment as a messenger for the *Dominica Guardian*. This is undoubtedly where he first met Joseph Hilton Steber,[23] the editor who was to become the stalwart patron of the local UNIA Division. He also became acquainted with Francis Louis Gardier, who taught him bookbinding. He would use this skill throughout his life to supplement his income. Characteristically, he kept meticulous records of his work,[24] some of which survive to this day. He recorded the date received, name of the client, title of the book, the nature of the work, the date delivered and the payment. Among his clients were the

Queen Street (now Victoria Street), Roseau, looking south.

managers of the Barclays Bank, the Royal Bank of Canada and business people, such as AC Shillingford, for whom he repaired or bound together ledgers and cash books connected with their business. He also put together the *Gazette* and Ordinances for the island's education department. Many of his clients had repairs carried out on prayer books and holy books or books associated with their work or particular interests such as dictionaries and compilations of music.

In 1918, Casimir got a job as a clerk with the highly respected and influential lawyer CEA Rawle. This was an important step in Casimir's career. This type of employment carried a certain status and marked him out as a white-collar worker. As a legal clerk he worked closely with his superiors and would be entrusted with confidential matters. Although the profession was not highly paid, it was regarded as a middle-class occupation.

During the years that followed his move to Roseau, Casimir became acutely aware of the discrimination and discrepancies within the society that he lived in. It was abundantly clear to him that power and privilege resided with the white colonialists and to a lesser extent with the mulatto elite. That intellect and aptitude mattered less than the options available by the virtue of heritage and pigmentation. It was also clear to him that there were few career opportunities available to ordinary black Dominicans like himself and that change was necessary.

3

Are We
Black-Bellied Reptiles?

It was the aftermath of the first world war that deepened Ralph Casimir's awareness of racism. The war may have been fought far away from Dominica, but many Dominicans signed up to fight for Britain. Lennox Honychurch attests that, by the middle of 1917, 'the island had sent more recruits than any other colony in the Leeward islands' and that most of those who went were labourers and the sons of small proprietors. Twenty-four Dominican lives were lost.[25] The war also brought economic hardship — fewer ships meant severe food shortages. More importantly, it alerted Casimir to the conditions endured by black soldiers fighting for the 'motherland' in Europe.

Casimir was an avid reader with an intense curiosity. His radicalisation resulted from both his own experiences, from his observations of how other Dominicans lived, and also from his reading about global affairs. Passionately interested in politics, both local and international, he preoccupied himself with historical inquiry, in particular to the past and present circumstances that affected the African diaspora.

Casimir learned that on their arrival in Europe the black soldiers of the British West Indian Regiment (BWIR), formed in 1915, were mainly assigned to the worst jobs. 'Arriving in the war zone, they found that the fighting was to be done by white soldiers, and that West Indians were to be assigned the dirty and dangerous work of loading ammunition, laying telephone wires and digging trenches. Most of

The racist treatment of black soldiers, many from the Caribbean, during the first world war, radicalised the young Casimir.

them went to war without guns.'[26] These volunteers had answered the call to serve 'only to find themselves discriminated against'.[27]

He had also read of the 1918 revolt of the BWIR at Taranto, in Italy, when BWIR soldiers were denied a pay rise given to other British troops on the basis that they had been classified as 'natives'. Tensions brought about by this sort of treatment eventually came to a head that December. 'Frustrated by their continued use as labourers while waiting for demobilisation, men of the 9th Battalion attacked their officers in a mutiny that lasted four days before being quelled.'[28]

Casimir also knew that black soldiers returning from war service found that there were few opportunities for employment, and that, in 1919, there were nine anti-black riots in British cities, in particular Cardiff and Liverpool, as former black soldiers, who had chosen to settle in Britain, competed for jobs with demobbed white soldiers. In Liverpool, for example, Charles Wooten, a sailor who had served in the war was killed by a mob in the docks.[29] A few days later, three West

Africans were stabbed in the street. Then, in mid-June of 1919, blacks were attacked by a white mob in Salford. They retaliated, and in the ensuing riots five people were killed.[30] There were also attacks on black servicemen, formerly of the British West Indies Regiment, in Cardiff. Other outbreaks of anti-black rioting took place in Glasgow and in London.[31] He had also read of the almost daily lynching of black people in the United States. He would have known that life in Dominica was hard for returning veterans and 'employment opportunities were scant, aside from backbreaking work' on the L Rose & Co lime estates.[32]

One of Casimir's earliest pieces of writing is an article for an unnamed newspaper entitled 'Race Prejudice', dated 24 September 1919. There, he railed against those who pretended the black man did not possess the same capacity of intellect or physical attributes as themselves. He asserted that 'Negroes from all parts of the world offered themselves to... White men's countries which were engaged in the Great War of Murders', and that they had sacrificed their lives for their cause. He proceeded to give examples of persecution in the Americas and also mentioned the British Negroes who, in post-war riots 'were massacred in the very heart of England'. So impassioned was Casimir by the situation that he declared 'DOWN WITH THE WHITE RACE'.[33]

It was such international injustices, alongside those that Casimir felt and saw around him, that motivated him to become an activist to try to bring about change and improvement for the ordinary Dominican. In 'Dominica and her Afric Sons', a poem written in 1922, he reflected:

> Thy sons have fought in the "War for Liberty?"
> Yet they have been deprived of dear "liberty."
> They have sacrificed themselves for old England
> And are now regarded as a worthless band.[34]

The post-war years brought the first stirrings of political reform in the Caribbean, especially among islands subject to Crown Colony rule. Dominica was no exception and, on 25 March 1919, the Representative Government Association (RGA) was founded by ARC Lockhart. (In the immediate post-war period, RGAs sprang up throughout the region and in other islands were often led by returning servicemen.)

In Dominica, the objective of the RGA was to press for an elected assembly and bring an end to the federation with the Leeward Islands which had not, it was argued, benefited Dominica. Public meetings were held at St Gerard's Hall in Roseau and attended by many people from all walks of life who came to listen to rousing speeches by Lockhart and CEA Rawle, by then Casimir's employer.[35] Casimir attended these gatherings and, after one such event, he wrote a letter to the *Dominica Guardian*, praising the speakers and bemoaning the fact that there had been little outward support from any of the merchants, planters or anyone with influence. He determined: 'Nothing is being done for the betterment of the poorer classes. Education is bad... The Government cannot afford... to supply the inhabitants with work... We should make a move... to send a petition to His Majesty the King praying for Representative Government.'[36] The recommendations from the RGA were put before the Legislative Council whose members voted unanimously in favour of reintroducing the elective principle to the local government. However the administrator directed the official members to vote against the motion, and as a result the motion was lost.

Responding to the growing ferment for political progress in their West Indian colonies, the British sent Major Edward Wood, under-secretary of state for the colonies, to the Caribbean. He arrived in Dominica in January 1922. While concerned that 70 per cent of the population was illiterate, he eventually gave his support to a limited elected legislature and in 1924 it was agreed that Dominica should have four elected members. The following year, the first elections since Crown colony rule were held. Those elected were CEA Rawle, AA Baron, HD Shillingford and SLV Green.[37]

It is most likely that it was around this time that Casimir began to describe himself as an African; eventually he would refer to himself and his United Negro Improvement Association (UNIA) colleagues as 'New Negroes'.[38] It was also at this point that he began to read the *Negro World*, the weekly newspaper founded by Marcus Garvey in New York during the first world war to promote the ideals and objectives of his landmark organisation, the UNIA. It stressed the importance of black pride and self-reliance urging all those of African descent to join the struggle for self-determination. Its message was clear and uncompromising.[39] In an interview many years later, Casimir said that his interest in the UNIA arose when he and two friends, Casimir Morancie, also known as 'the Patois Orator', a tailor born in Bellevue Chopin, a village in southern Dominica, and the bookbinder Francis Louis Gardier, began to read the *Negro World*.[40] There were many Dominicans living in the United States at the time and copies of the newspaper could have arrived in Dominica as fellow Dominicans sent letters home. It was widely circulated: at its peak it sold 200,000 copies across the African diaspora, to powerful effect and the alarm of colonial officials.[41]

The UNIA remains the most impressive of all Pan-African political movements. Its influence was undeniable on the architects of the West Indian Federation, the subsequent independence of Caribbean island states as well as the Civil Rights and Black Power movements in the US. Its aims were: 'to establish a brotherhood among the black race; to promote a spirit of race pride; to reclaim the fallen and to assist the backward tribes of Africa.' Its motto: 'One Aim. One God. One Destiny.'

Marcus Garvey, *Provisional President of Africa*
founder of
Universal Negro Improvement Association
and African Communities League
On the Black Star Line.

Marcus Garvey: the emblem of the Black Star Line is on his lapel.

Marcus Garvey (1887-1940) had been born in Jamaica, a decade before Casimir. He, too, had worked in the print industry, and it was as a young man that he became aware of the discrimination suffered by his fellow black Jamaicans. His leadership skills were first tested as a trade unionist and he would lose his job as a result of this political activism.

Emigrating to Costa Rica in 1910, Garvey took up employment with the United Fruit Company along with many other West Indians on the banana plantations. His job was that of timekeeper, to ensure the smooth running of the 'factory in the fields'. Although he only spent a few months on the plantations he was disquieted by the bullying and belittling he witnessed of his fellow West Indians. In his short time in Costa Rica, he published a bilingual newspaper, *The Nation/La Nación*, and used it to target the West Indian colonial leadership. He went on to spend time as an itinerant worker in Honduras, Ecuador, Colombia,

Venezuela and Panama. Working on the Panama Canal, he experienced at first hand the 'Jim Crow' standards and segregation practised by the US contractors[42] and other examples of discrimination in employment.

In 1912, he was in London where he immersed himself in political reading, polished his public speaking and rubbed shoulders with the leaders of various radical movements. It was there that he came across the *African Times and Orient Review,* owned by the Egyptian Duse Mohammed Ali. Garvey was taken on by the newspaper as a messenger and handyman. However, always on the look out for self-advancement, it was not long before he was given an opportunity to write for the *Review.* His first piece was a historical essay, 'The British West Indies in the Mirror of Civilization.'[43] The focus of the article was on the excesses and greed of the European in the Caribbean and how colour was a barrier to advancement and employment opportunities in Jamaica.

Garvey returned to Jamaica in 1914 and claimed that it was during the three-week boat journey back home, with time to reflect and plan, that he resolved to set up the organisation which would become the Universal Negro Improvement Association (UNIA). His sojourn in England and Europe had 'sharpened Garvey's belief in his own destiny and heightened his sense of racial awareness.'[44]

Like Casimir, Garvey believed that the first world war had radicalised black people. He noted that recruitment to the UNIA was helped along by the war in raising the consciousness of the black US soldiers who were good enough to fight but were barred from becoming officers.

By 1919, and in the years that followed, the UNIA became a mass movement throughout the Caribbean, cutting across political and linguistic barriers with branches in more than a dozen islands. Some islands boasted multiple branches: there were 52, for example, in

Cuba, 30 in Trinidad and 11 in Jamaica.[45] Dominica, under the leadership of Ralph Casimir, would establish five branches.

Casimir first wrote to Garvey asking for support in setting up a branch of the UNIA in Dominica in June 1919 but he received no reply. Undeterred, Casimir persisted and sent a steady stream of letters between October 1919 and April 1920 to Garvey, the UNIA and the *Negro World*. With no further response from that quarter, he turned to REM Jack, a Garveyite in St Vincent, who had already set up a UNIA branch there.[46] With his encouragement and support, Casimir transformed the newly formed Dominican Brotherhood Union (DBU) into a branch of the UNIA and, by the time a response finally arrived from Marcus Garvey in May 1920, the DBU had already set its course.

In the 'Dominica Report'[47] of 5 July 1920, Ralph Casimir reported to the UNIA annual conference, held at its headquarters in Harlem in New York, that, in 1919 he and his two friends, Morancie and Gardier, had been influenced by an article in the *Negro World*, and, fired up with enthusiasm, resolved to form an organisation to fight what they saw as the discrimination against ordinary people in their society. Thus the DBU, an organisation which became amalgamated with Garvey's UNIA, was born. Once recognised by the parent body of the UNIA, the DBU became the official UNIA Division #85 in Dominica. In its armoury were the weapons of disciplined organisation of political activity, the spoken and the written word. The three men were soon joined by Herbert Severin, a pharmacist, who later emigrated to the US to complete his studies. and Henry Elwin, a Post Office clerk. Together they created and signed the following pledge:

Dated at Roseau, Dominica B.W.I.
On the 9th day of January AD 1920
THE NEGRO TO HELP THE NEGRO
We hereby sincerely and truly pledge to give our support, and we

are quite ready at any moment to shed our blood and to give our very lives to this cause and shall do all what lies in our power to help one and all members of the race who is for this good and just cause.

We vow that We are sincerely and truly New Negroes. So help us God

Francis Louis Gardier (President)

Herbert David Severin (Vice President)

JR Ralph Casimir (Secretary & Treasurer)

Casimir Morancie (Assistant Secretary)

Henry J Elwin (Board Member)[48]

That same day, the founding meeting of the Dominica UNIA Charter #85 was held on the upper floor of a building in Roseau owned by Victor L Ducreay, a shopkeeper and liquor seller.[49] It was

Casimir's UNIA membership certificate, June 1921, showing his position as secretary, with his mother and sister in charge of the Ladies' Division.

attended by 12 members. The second meeting, held two weeks later, on 23 January, in St Gerard's Hall, Roseau, received extensive coverage in the *Dominica Guardian*. Regarded as a 'coloured' newspaper, it reported that there were 150 people in the packed hall with others crowding outside. As well as Casimir, speakers at the meeting included Gardier, and Dr CC Ligouri, a UNIA sympathiser and visitor to the island on his way to Halifax, Canada (described in the newspaper as a 'distinguished Negro visitor'). Joseph Steber, the long-standing editor of the *Dominica Guardian*, chaired the meeting. Dr Ligouri reminded the audience of the importance of pride in the Negro race and traced a history featuring black heroes of the achievements and progress made since the days of slavery. He also stressed the importance of education, the hope and promise of the future, and upheld Marcus Mosiah Garvey, as 'independent, intelligent and fearless' and the champion of the Negro race. He urged them to live in unity and believed that all, even the 'well-to-do coloured people' would eventually rally to the cause.

Steber spoke of the reality of the Black Star Line in the form of the *SS Frederick Douglass*, the first vessel to be launched. This was a reference to the steamship corporation set up by Marcus Garvey to facilitate the transportation of goods by African Americans. Eventually, it was hoped it would also transport people throughout the African diaspora. Now Negroes 'may not submit any longer to the insults and indignities' to which they had been previously subjected while travelling. He gave a personal example of this. He then spoke of the treatment black soldiers had received in England returning from the war in comparison to that of French Negroes. Gardier urged those present to rally to the Association as a 'means of combatting the injustices' they were subjected to by those who 'harboured an impression of racial superiority'. Casimir read out a formal message which would be sent to Marcus Garvey. Conrad Alleyne, one of the supporters, gave a vote of thanks and the meeting ended with 'lusty cheers' from the audience.[50]

In 1893, in the wake of the La Plaine riots in which four Dominicans had been killed in a protest over taxation,[51] three men — ARC Lockhart,[52] William Davies[53] and Sholto Rawlins Pemberton[54] — had founded the *Dominica Guardian* 'to keep guard over the interests of our people.'[55] They chose Joseph Steber, the son of a German seaman and a Dominican woman,[56] to manage and edit the paper. These men also founded the 'Party of Progress', an organisation 'which represented the views of the progressive section of the coloured population on the island.'[57] While the Party of Progress represented affluent members of the mulatto elite,[58] the UNIA leadership came mainly from the petit bourgeoisie and working class, and was dominated by small independent traders and the self-employed. Apart from the original signatures at the formation of the UNIA, other supporters were JC Wyke, a butcher, and Sidney Green, a pharmacist (the latter would become an elected member of the Legislative Council in 1925).

Membership of the UNIA grew quickly. Six months after its formation, it exceeded 800. With its headquarters in Roseau, there were soon branches in many parts of the island: in Soufriere, Pointe Michel, Grand Bay in the south, and, one of the biggest, in Marigot, in the north-east. A report on the activities of the UNIA in Dominica by Inspector John Skirving of the Leeward Island Police to Robert Walter, the then administrator in Dominica, states that there was a 'joining fee of 25 cents and weekly subscription 3d, and members are led to expect monetary and medical benefits when sick... So far the fees and subscriptions appear to be used only for the payment of rent and lighting expenses of the meeting place.'[59] He also noted that the membership were in the main young people and doubted that it would have longevity.

The Casimir family were all involved in the UNIA. His mother Maria and sister Meredith became extremely active Garveyites. Both women held positions on the committee of the Roseau division. Maria, who was nicknamed 'Mama Black Star Line', was lady president and Meredith was lady general secretary. His brother Hubert was also an active member but held no official position. Hubert took the view that the surname 'Casimir' was one which he no longer wanted to use as it had been that of a slave owner. Instead, he began to use his middle name George as his surname.[60]

The Dominica branch of the UNIA took up the ideals of self-help and racial pride in all parts of its members' lives. It embraced an extraordinary broad base of activities. For example, it maintained a

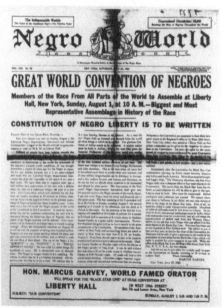

A front page of Negro World, *the mouthpiece of the UNIA, July 1920. Casimir was a frequent contributor in prose and poetry.*

Black Cross Nurses division, which was modelled on the Red Cross. Although only a few women may have had formal nursing training, their role was to provide health services and hygiene education and to give practical support in nutrition and infant care to the members of their community. Dominica's UNIA set up a supplementary school,[61] organised by Maria Casimir, where youngsters could learn about their African heritage and African history. This would have been the first of its kind on the island. The UNIA also ran a literary society which met for poetry readings, staged plays and held debates.[62] The Division's income from subscriptions was used to support members through a 'mutual aid or friendly society, paying sick and death benefits to members'.[63] Members knew that should they fall ill or have a sudden bereavement they would benefit from this arrangement.

One of Casimir's major roles in the UNIA as secretary was to send reports to the *Negro World* about its activities, and about the political issues and context of life in Dominica (he also sent the newspaper many of his poems). In his initial report to the UNIA of 5 July 1920,[64] Casimir indicated that there was unrest among the people of the island due to 'unnecessary prohibitive laws, high rates of exchange, high costs of living, low wages, profiteering, poor educational system, a lack of steamship communication, need for a coastal steamer, inland communication...' He laid these ills at the door of Crown Colony rule and compared the wages of workers in Dominica to those of workers in similar types of occupations in England. 'White man, must the Negro labourer in Dominica starve, stay in rags or naked, while the pale face labourer is well fed and clothed?'[65] He said of the more affluent: 'The-well-to-do Negroes are crooks. They don't care a pin about the UNIA but are clamouring for agency of the Black Star Line.'

In his criticism of the education system in Dominica, he maintained that it was one of the worst among the West Indian islands. He accused the government of failing to enforce compulsory education and of discriminating against Negroes by failing to give opportunities to pupil teachers to further their education. He may well have been reflecting on his own personal experience.

An earlier, hard-hitting essay, 'What Ails Dominica', had been published in the *Negro World* on 26 April 1920 and later in the *West Indian Times*. There, Casimir was particularly interested in describing how problematic it was for black people to travel, both around Dominica and, internationally, to and from North America. At home, he drew attention to the lack of transport around the island. 'People [in Dominica] have to make long journeys by means of small native canoes... Long journeys in such a small craft are very dangerous during storms.' He wrote of an almost non-existent inland road network and pointed out that produce could only be transported by 'beasts of burden, and... carried by the people on their head or backs...' He ended by promoting the UNIA as an organ 'to promote race pride... to assist the needy, to work for better conditions among our people in Dominica...'[66] The article made a deep impression upon the readers of the *Negro World*. Following its publication, the newspaper received letters from members in other West Indian islands speaking of 'a deep sense of gratitude and admiration for articulating what many people in the Caribbean had been feeling but unable to express'.[67]

Casimir also drew attention to the treatment of Negro passengers travelling on the Quebec Line, both within the Caribbean region and to and from the United States. Thus he became a keen supporter of Garvey's brain child, the Black Star Line. Often referred to as providing a means for taking black people back to Africa, the Black Star Line was more likely to have been a response to the injustice of segregation suffered by black passengers. It was well known that black and coloured people who travelled with first-class tickets on the Cunard shipping lines and the White Star Line were summarily relegated to third class and could only expect to be served a meal after the white passengers had dined.[68] Garvey saw his shipping line as a chance for black people, who wished to travel in dignity and in the luxury of first class, to do just so.

The Black Star Line may have been a major reason for the growth of support in Dominica for the UNIA. In a letter to Garvey, in May 1920, Casimir wrote: 'We hope that the Black Star Line will soon pass here. She will get many passengers as the negroes here who are desirous of leaving for the States cannot easily obtain passage in the white man's steamers.'[69] Travel to and from Dominica was notoriously difficult. There were two steamers of the Quebec Line which regularly travelled to the Caribbean from New York or Halifax, in Canada. Yet ordinary West Indians found it difficult to secure a passage. They would sometimes have to wait up to a year before being accepted. When allowed to travel, they were not treated well. Steber, for example, in his address to the UNIA meeting on 23 January 1920, had spoken of the disagreeable treatment he had suffered while aboard the SS *Parima*, of the Quebec Line.

During 1920, Casimir became the official agent for the Black Star Line in Dominica He was granted this franchise as secretary of the local UNIA division, and, since he was already well known to the organisation, the usual references and surety bond of $20.00 were also dispensed with.[70] He also had permission to sell stock for the Inter-Colonial Steamship and Trading Company. Many investors, encouraged by Casimir's involvement, were attracted by the offer, and Dominicans bought hundreds of shares in the Black Star Line. Many who bought shares were small trades people: shoemakers, seamstresses, shopkeepers, and peasant cultivators who were attracted by its 'promise to provide them with their "own" shipping.'[71] A number of prominent Dominicans, including JB Charles, the father of Eugenia Charles, prime minister of Dominica from 1980 to 1995, also bought shares in the Black Star Line. While some investors did not necessarily support the UNIA, they saw it as a lucrative opportunity.

Such stirrings had not gone unnoticed by the colonial authorities in the Caribbean. The British government feared the influence of black nationalism emanating from the United States would influence their subjects in the colonies,[72] and, in March 1920, an effort was made to ban the circulation of the *Negro World* in its West Indian and African colonies through the Seditious Publications Ordinance, which carried a fine of £100 or ten years' imprisonment. Seen as a direct attack on Casimir and his followers, it was not passed by the Legislative Council in Dominica. Rawle was among those who opposed the bill. Interestingly, it did become law in many other West Indian islands and, also, in the then Gold Coast (Ghana) thus resulting in the banning of the *Negro World*. It was at this point that Casimir took up the role as the clandestine supplier to subscribers of the paper on other islands and the Gold Coast. The banned newspapers were smuggled in by willing black seamen and other sympathisers.

When Casimir had begun to distribute the *Negro World* in December 1919, his client base was 25. By the time of the introduction of the Seditious Publications Ordinance, it had doubled. By July 1920, circulation 'had surpassed four hundred, making Garvey's weekly the most widely read newspaper in Dominica'.[73] And it was Casimir and the UNIA who organised that year's Emancipation celebrations (see chapter 4), a landmark event in the story of the UNIA in Dominica.

The ruling elite in Dominica were also well aware of the activities of the UNIA and were not in favour of what they saw. In one effort, for example, to hinder and disrupt support for the Black Star Line, a cap was put on the amount of money that could be spent on a postal order; this was the means used to send subscriptions and money for the purchase of shares in the Black Star Line to the UNIA headquarters. The authorities ruled that no one could acquire a postal order for more than £2.00 within a fortnight.[74]

Apart from the attack on the distribution of the *Negro World*, Casimir himself faced further opposition from Dominica's powerful bourgeoisie. Despite the fact that Rawle had opposed the suppression of the *Negro* World, he wrote to Casimir on 26 August 1920 stating that he would either have to cease his political activities or seek new employment. Rawle pointed out that his clients, among them affluent landowners, had threatened to stop using him as their lawyer if Casimir, seen by some of them as a troublemaker, continued to work for him.

Rawle's letter stated: 'In reply to your request for leave from the 28th, I find it necessary to dispense with your services entirely during the month of September. Your recent political activities and speeches have given great offence to the majority of my clients both white and coloured, many of whom threaten to withdraw their work from me if I continue to employ you. These articles and speeches have been exceedingly offensive in tone and stupid in manner, and certainly in no way help the cause which you profess to champion. While I cannot and do not intend to control your political views, I am certainly not going to allow my practice or my reputation to be injured by your buffoonery.

'A month's rest will I have decided do you a lot of good. If at the end of the month you are in a more sober frame of mind, and undertake to refrain from political or radical activities of every description, I will gladly re-employ you.'[75]

In response to this ultimatum, Casimir chose to leave Rawle's employment, and left his job at the end of August. He would support himself on the stipend he received as a cantor at Roseau Cathedral and his work as a freelance bookbinder.

Meanwhile, all was not well with Dominica's UNIA branch. While there was no question as to its efficient administration and scrupulous records, financial troubles began to beset the organisation. At the beginning of 1921, Gardier, the UNIA's local president, was accused by members of misappropriating funds. We do not know the circumstances but it is clear that Casimir took exception to Gardier's behaviour. In February of that year, he wrote to Gardier stating that he could no longer maintain their friendship and told him in no uncertain terms that he was 'not fit to be even a member of this greatest and blessed organisation for Negro Upliftment'.[76]

Later, in June of that year, Casimir travelled to Trinidad in his capacity as UNIA representative to oversee and report back on the activities and issues of the Trinidadian UNIA chapters. Prior to his departure, Casimir received a letter from his UNIA division expressing their 'appreciation for services rendered' to the cause and describing him as 'industrious and diligent'. The letter, signed by Gardier, who was still serving as President, and the officers of the Division, ran: 'We can never forget the day you... abandoned your employment to stick to the UNIA, that caused us to believe the more in you.'[77]

Casimir's first stop in Trinidad was to Guaico, a community in the north-east of Trinidad. Invited by Edward CA Philip, who ran the division with his wife, Mary, and son, Isaiah, Casimir supported the unveiling and establishment of this UNIA chapter. The branch numbered some 100 members, and, on Casimir's advice, a unit of Black Cross nurses and of the Universal African Legions was formed. The latter comprised ex-military men, headed by Elbert Morancie, a former member of the British West Indies Regiment.[78] Casimir also reported on his visits to other Trinidadian towns. At Tabaquite, for example, he was concerned that money was being sent to a James Braithwaite, linked to the International Working Men's Association, erroneously believing that he was the head of the UNIA in Trinidad; the money collected for the sale of shares in the Black Star Line, Casimir reported, was not properly accounted for. At Brothers Road, a very new but well-organised chapter of 75 members, he spoke to the members about organisational matters. He also addressed the unit at Penal where he was annoyed to find a pastor claiming to represent the UNIA church.[79] On visiting St Joseph, he found that the organiser had ordered supplies from New York and resold them to the membership at greatly increased prices for personal profit. He was most impressed with the La Brea division where he delivered a speech. In his report to the parent body he advised that a 'leader for these islands (Trinidad, St Vincent, St Lucia and Dominica) should be stationed in Barbados.'[80] A full report was sent to the UNIA headquarters and published in the *Negro World* in September 1921.

On his return to Dominica on 18 August 1921,[81] some weeks after that year's Emancipation celebrations (see chapter 4), Casimir received a letter from JC Wyke, acting president general and the executive member of the Dominica Division, welcoming him back and congratulating him on the success of his trip. The letter also informed him that Gardier had resigned from his role as president and that Casimir had been duly elected to replace him.

Casimir's high energy levels for writing remained undimmed. For several months in 1921, he ran a column in the *Barbados Times* called 'Notes From Dominica' under the pseudonym Civis Africanus. In February of that year he reported that a number of children between the ages of 12 to 14 years were brought before the Magistrates Court to answer charges for not paying road tax. He remarks, 'Such is the case of Crown Colony rule (slavery in disguise).'[82] In other articles that have survived, he reported on the issues around taxation, the public meetings held and was vehement with his opinions, claiming that 'Dominica has only selfish leaders — intellectual parasites — who do things for their own individual welfare.'[83] In April, he wrote about the 'War Tax' being imposed on islanders and that a census was due in a few days which he was certain would show that the population had decreased due to the number who had left since the last census.[84] In another of his 'Notes', he complains that the RGA are 'chicken hearted soldiers — weak-kneed leaders have surrendered in the fight'.[85] Included was a poem which praised Dominica for its beauty and ended:

> Awake sons of patriotic Dominica!
> Ye are the offspring of Africa
> Let not these selfish pale faces,
> Regard ye as inferior men.[86]

The UNIA was not the only black organisation of the time: the African Blood Brotherhood (ABB) and the National Association for the Advancement of Colored People (NAACP) were also significant movements. The NAACP, founded in 1910, was led by the Harvard-educated intellectual WEB Dubois while the ABB, formed in 1918, was headed by Cyril Briggs, an African American of British and Caribbean heritage who described himself as a Marxist. Both organisations had an uneasy relationship with the UNIA.

Initially, there was some cooperation between the movements, but inevitably the two organisations came into conflict with the UNIA, most notably the ABB. When the ABB was invited to attend the UNIA Second International Convention of the Negro Peoples of the World in 1921, Garvey was badgered into giving a platform to the ABB's wealthy, white communist supporter, Rose Pastor Stokes, despite there being no previous precedent for giving a platform to a white person as this was an international convention of Negroes. It soon became clear that the ABB's agenda was to infiltrate and appropriate the membership of the UNIA. There were disruptions of various kinds from the floor and ABB members began to distribute what purported to be a news bulletin of conference events, which served to contribute to criticism of the UNIA's affairs, which were reproduced in other black newspapers. The final straw for Garvey was 'the sight of its vendors hawking the (anti-Garvey) *Chicago Defender* on the steps of Liberty Hall'.[87] This resulted in the expulsion of ABB members from the convention; Garvey stated that Briggs was 'the paid servant of certain destructive white elements which aimed at exploiting Negroes for their own subservient needs'.[88] Garvey also accused Briggs of being a white man masquerading as a Negro which led to a libel suit against him, which Briggs won.

Casimir corresponded with both Dubois and Briggs, and also subscribed to their publications — the NAACP's *Crisis* and the ABB's *Crusader*. These fed Casimir's thirst for knowledge, his insatiable appetite for ideas and avenues to uplift the Negro race. In an article, published on 16 September 1921 in the *Crusader*, entitled 'A Stirling Call for Co-operation and Race Loyalty',[89] Casimir asserts, 'These papers teach us a great deal about the glories of our Race and if we follow them closely we will act as men and won't allow any so called superior race to treat us as "black bellied reptiles".[90] He calls for unity and respect towards the leaders of the respective groups. He also reminds readers about the leading black figures in the Gold Coast, Britain and the Caribbean, signing off 'Yours for a United Negro Race'.[91]

Casimir's approach was not supported by the UNIA leadership. A letter from Fred Toole, the UNIA's secretary general in Harlem, instructed him that 'on no account must any members of the organisation associate with this body [ABB]'. Toole went on to say that the ABB were in the pay of supporters of Bolshevism, had nothing in common with the UNIA and were engaged in undermining their organisation through the *Crusader*.[92] A letter to Casimir from Briggs[93] in October of that year certainly appears to support this assertion. Briggs' letter outlined the issues being faced by the UNIA with regards to the Black Star Line. He claims that the ABB is a secret organisation based upon 'secret organising and quiet preparation for the tremendous task ahead' and implies that they have infiltrated certain enterprises. He also writes that the ABB has 'reliable information brought us by members of the ABB who are also members of the UNIA and employed in the offices' dealing with the BSL'.

It is clear that there were members of the ABB working within various key enterprises of the UNIA reporting back to Briggs and providing key information about the financial state of the UNIA. The tone of the letter implies that the UNIA is not fit for purpose, and although he believes in 'the spectacular feature of the enterprise — Negro ships on all the seven seas — it's the tactics employed to achieve this are at fault'. Briggs believed in the project but was critical of the strategies employed by the UNIA. He stated that it had been an error to begin a business enterprise that needed support from the white man in the early stages and 'be in fact at the mercy of the white man who dominates that line of business'. Briggs also states that the ABB has no real foothold in the Caribbean and suggests that Casimir could help to restore morale and 'help to educate the negro in proper tactics'.[94] There is no record of Casimir's response.

Following the events of the previous months, the Dominica Division, now with Casimir as president, dusted themselves off from the difficulties created by Gardier. A letter from the Penal Division in Trinidad made it clear that Gardier's transgression had become common knowledge. The writer expressed sympathy that there had been 'a rascal' among the members; he went on to say that similar problems had been identified in Penal and two other Trinidadian Divisions. On a more personal note, he hoped that Casimir, who had been unwell for a time during the previous months, had recovered.[95]

For a time Casimir attempted to fill both roles as general president and general secretary, but he was soon informed by the UNIA'S parent body in New York that it was unconstitutional so to do.[96] However, from the evidence available, it is clear that Casimir continued to organise the five Divisions on the island travelling around Dominica extensively, recruiting members and shareholders for the Black Star Line. It says much for his skills and dedication that Dominica was regarded as the UNIA's 'strongest outpost in the English-speaking Caribbean'[97] based on the efficiency and quality of its functioning.

In an article, written on 21 December 1921, and published in the *Negro World* in the New Year,[98] Casimir's philosophy is trenchantly stated: 'Before you pass away from this world it is your duty to do all that is in your power to help our struggling down-trodden race. Remember you shall pass through this world but once. Any good thing therefore, that you can do or any kindness you can show to any member of the race, do it now. Defer not nor neglect it, for you shall not pass this way again.'[99]

Casimir called on all Negroes to unite together no matter their colour,[100] to stop thinking negatively about themselves and their abilities. Readers were reminded of the achievements of Negroes of the past as well as the riches of the continent of Africa. In a few sentences, Casimir demonstrated the breadth of his knowledge on the subject. He urged them to carry on the fight for freedom and cited various examples, including 'Ireland, whose people have been struggling for centuries... our fore-parents during the days of slavery fought hard for freedom and died without enjoying even the partial freedom that we enjoy today.' He wrote of the importance of the struggle for the future of their children and grandchildren, that it was through the UNIA that progress for the race would be achieved.[101]

It is not difficult to imagine that such fervour exemplified all his dealings with the UNIA branches in Dominica. However, the Dominica UNIA was yet again facing a turbulent time. Unsurprisingly, money was at the root of the matter and it was at this point that the organisation began to unravel. Gardier's misappropriation of funds had already cast a shadow on the integrity of the organisation. Casimir reported to Professor Tony Martin, who interviewed him many years later, that those who had benefited financially from the mutual aid benevolent fund often took advantage of the situation and stopped paying their dues once they had recovered from illness.[102]

Despite Casimir's efforts to hold the organisation together, the membership had become restless. There was no sign of the promised Black Star Line in which many had so faithfully invested. The dream was beginning to evaporate and Casimir felt harried on all sides by the membership who believed they had been let down both by him and by the UNIA. In mid-1922 he wrote to New York several times explaining the situation and requesting them to send a high-ranking official to help him to resolve the issues that plagued the UNIA in Dominica.

The reply from Enid Lumos, the secretary for the UNIA, was not helpful: 'Your many letters requesting that an Executive Officer of the Parent Body be sent to visit your Division have been received, but you will understand that Dominica is very far from the United States of America, and it is not possible to send Officers to your Division, as it is to send them to Divisions in the United States of America.'[103] She suggested that as the Reverend Torbitt, an executive member of the UNIA, was resident in Barbados, he could be called on for assistance. Their priority at the time was to prepare for the annual UNIA Convention which was weeks away. Casimir's UNIA division was not the only one fighting for survival. HN Huggins, UNIA president general in St Vincent, in a letter to Casimir confided, 'I am struggling, my Division is flat on the ground.' He, too, hoped for a visit from the 'parent body'. 'I am hearing so many different things, had I not courage I would fail already.'[104]

Garvey was by this point facing problems of his own. It is not surprising that Garvey's activities had come to the notice of the US government. Targeted by J Edgar Hoover, who hired the first black FBI agent to spy on him in 1919, he was accused of mail fraud: a brochure, advertising the Black Star Line, included the photograph of a ship, the *SS Phyllis Wheatley*, which had not yet been acquired, was central to the allegation. This coupled with financial mismanagement of funds did not bode well. Garvey ill-advisedly chose to conduct his own defence. He had no previous legal experience and was convicted of fraud in 1923 and sentenced to five years' imprisonment. Following numerous appeals, and a realisation that 'the prosecution was designed for the protection of coloured people' and the fact that 'none of these people apparently believe they have been defrauded',[105] Garvey was pardoned by President Calvin Coolidge and deported to Jamaica on 3 December 1927. A crowd of thousands, waving and crying, gathered at the dock in New Orleans to pay their respects at his departure.

Back in Dominica, Casimir had been unable to hold the fracturing Dominica Division together and without support from the troubled UNIA parent body, Casimir resigned as president and also from Dominica's UNIA Division in early 1923. Many years later, he was to confide to Lennox Honychurch that he had felt caught in the middle of an unsolvable situation between the local membership and New York.[106] He felt that the ground had slipped away from him. A prime impetus for his supporters had always been the possibility of the Black Star Line and, as that faded away, they were anxious to know of the fate of their investment and what resolutions might be forthcoming. Casimir had no answers to pass on.

Casimir wrote to inform Marcus Garvey and his wife Amy Jacques Garvey of his resignation. In his letter he stated that 'certain rascals are trying to break what others are working hard to build'. He received a long and moving response from Jacques Garvey in which she asserted, 'This condition has existed since the inception of the

Organisation, and will continue... Some Negroes have always been accustomed to tell "Massa Boss", and to sell out their race. It is very hard for us to absolutely change this habit that has imbibed us since Slavery. We can only make attempts to counteract this evil under the rule of Alien Government.' She encouraged him to take courage and continue to fight the cause of the UNIA for the 'upliftment' of the Negro. She wrote that she had shown the letter to her husband who had wanted to know the reasons for Casimir's resignation as president of the Dominica UNIA. Her letter ended on a poignant note: 'I, who have more to bear than you do, am not discouraged. Why should you be? Take more hope.'[107]

Although he did not continue in the leadership role that the Garveys requested, Casimir's own personal commitment and interaction with the UNIA remained staunch. He continued to contribute to the *Negro World* and to make personal financial contributions to the UNIA. When Marcus Garvey visited Dominica in 1937, it was Casimir who organised the proceedings (see chapter 5).

While Casimir's direct association with the UNIA in Dominica lasted for only three years, he was regarded as 'one of the most influential and hard-working UNIA figures in the West Indies'.[108] He had travelled to support the organisation, formed strong bonds with other UNIA activists in the region and world wide, and offered support and advice to the organisers of newer divisions. This brief period had given Dominicans a sense of pride in the dignity of their own history and heritage. During those important years of 1919 to 1923, Dominica held 'a pivotal role in the most successful Pan-African movement'[109] and 'enjoyed a central role in Caribbean political development',[110] thereby setting a course for political freedom that would come many decades later.

4
Songs of Freedom

Emancipation Day celebrations described in this chapter were arranged by the UNIA Dominica Division and took place in Roseau on 1 and 2 August 1920[111] and, in the following year, by Joseph Steber in Soufriere, on 1 August 1921. I have tried to give life to the thoughts and feelings that Ralph Casimir would have experienced and to convey the atmosphere. My account is based on reports of the events, which appeared in the Dominica Guardian, and as interpreted from interviews with Ralph Casimir in the 1980s.

Emancipation Day procession during celebrations in Roseau in 1920 organised by Casimir and the local UNIA Division.

The 1920 event was more extensive than anything that had taken place previously and it was the first time that the celebrations had been planned and executed by a group of ordinary Dominicans. This occasion was probably the highpoint of the UNIA's organisation in Dominica.

Dominica's Emancipation celebrations began on 1 August 1920 at 3pm when the members of the Roseau UNIA Division #85 gathered together for the 'Unfurling of the Flag' — the silken green, red and black UNIA flag, designed by Marcus Garvey. It had been a gift from Dominican members of the UNIA in Harlem. The ceremony was held at the building the UNIA members had christened Liberty Hall, the spacious premises above VL Ducreay's shop in New Street, which the organisation rented for its thrice weekly meetings. The meeting had opened with a rendition of 'From Greenland's Icy Mountains'. Well known to missionaries, it spoke of a commitment to the Christianisation of Africa and Asia and was the official opening hymn for all UNIA events in Dominica, the US and wherever else in the world there was a UNIA Division.

> From Greenland's icy mountains,
> From India's coral strand,
> Where Afric's sunny fountains
> Roll down their golden sand,
> From many an ancient river,
> From many a palmy plain,
> They call us to deliver
> Their land from error's chain.[112]

Francis Gardier, the president, began with an address on the importance of the flag for the UNIA and Africans; as other nations had their own national emblems so should Africans. The officers and members had solemnly exited the hall with the flag tightly rolled. Then everyone had stood around on the pavement to watch the flag unfurled, accompanied by hearty cheers from members and the passersby who lingered to watch the ceremony.

Joseph Steber was in attendance and spoke of the significance of the ceremony. He referred to Garvey's comment, 'Show me a race or nation without a flag, and I will show you a race of people without any pride.'[113] Steber reiterated the importance of respecting the flag and of being prepared to defend its integrity with their lives. He spoke about the symbolism of the flag's colours: black represented the noble and distinguished race to which all those of African descent belong, red, the blood which had already been shed and must be spilt in pursuit of redemption and liberty while green signified hope, the luxuriant vegetation and natural wealth of Africa.[114] He said that Africans had accomplished much in the short span of time since their 'ancestors had been freed by the most gracious act of Victoria the Good',[115] and there was hope for much brighter futures. Pledges for unity and support of Marcus Garvey were followed by a vigorous rendition of *Africa Our Home*.[116] They also sang the song which became known as the UNIA's National Anthem, the 'Universal Ethiopian Anthem', composed by Arnold Ford, the UNIA's musical director, and his associate Benjamin Burrel, with its chorus:

> Advance, advance to victory,
> Let Africa be free;
> Advance to meet the foe
> With the might
> Of the red, the black and the green[117]

Garvey's followers believed music to be an effective medium through which to spread their message of Negro empowerment and

Members of the cast of the Grand Variety Entertainment,
August 1920, in their UNIA sashes. Casimir seated (left)
with his mother (standing) behind his sister
Meredith (seated).

racial uplift. With a focus primarily on content rather than form, UNIA musicians gave voice to the organisation's agenda through spirituals, jazz, blues and choral arrangements.[118]

Ralph Casimir would have been pleased with the events of the day but would have thought that the celebrations of 2 August even more significant; the event had been advertised in the *Dominica Guardian* for weeks and the members were hoping for a strong turnout.

The whole Casimir family joined those assembled for the parade and would have been relieved to see how many people had turned up.

Casimir Morancie and Herbert Severin unfurled the large silken UNIA banner as Ralph Casimir and his fellow leaders, with their official UNIA sashes and caps of red, green and black, directed the gathering throng. They marched behind the band up Great George Street and along Great Marlborough Street on the roughly paved road between an array of wooden housing, some *ti kais* and some more elaborate structures in the French colonial style with overhanging verandas and galvanised roofs. People came out on to their verandas and others began to line the streets. Some joined in the gaiety by attaching themselves to the back of the parade and, as it proceeded up Queen Mary Street and on to Constitution Hill, a carnival atmosphere took over. The procession rounded into Virgin Lane, passing the Bishop's Palace on the left, with its resplendent flamboyant trees, and hedges of pink bougainvillea crowding over the iron railings.

Ahead was the Graeco-Roman cathedral, Our Lady of Fair Haven, dominating Roseau from the hilltop on which it stood. Fashioned from local stone and with three steeples designed to impress, it was built over a period of more than a century by volunteers determined to ensure that they would have an appropriate Catholic place of worship.[119] The procession, headed by the local UNIA leaders, marched up the carriage way and climbed the steep steps before entering its broad aisle; they genuflected before dispersing into the pews.

The priests entered in their robes of white, green and gold signifying hope followed by the acolytes in procession to the high altar. The choir master raised his baton. The organ sprang to life and the congregation raised their voices as they sung 'Veni Creator'. Casimir's voice rose in unison with the choir, up into the flying buttresses and beyond. The congregation was exhilarated by the high Mass and a thousand voices were raised in prayer and song, and united in purpose. Throughout, Casimir led the congregation as cantor with the high Mass being sung by the Redemptorist Belgian priests, Reverend Father Van Der Westerlaken, supported by his compatriots Father de Ridder and Father Morris.

After the thanksgiving Mass, the congregation paraded through the town again swirling both the Union Jack and UNIA flag. We might wonder at this apparent paradox. However, there was no contradiction for the UNIA members. Their alliance to the UNIA flag was an assertion of their belief in themselves as proud British Negroes who also believed and celebrated their allegiance to 'The Mother Country' and firmly believed themselves to be British subjects. They 'marched through the streets... witnessed by hundreds of sightseers and followed by an immense crowd. Possibly about 1000 persons were in the procession.'[120] As the procession went along Turkey Lane and turned right towards the sea front, the band struck up a new tune. The parade then turned into King George V Street and the marchers were elated by the hundreds of sightseers who lined the route. Once again, they climbed up Constitution Hill propelled by the buoyant tune of 'When the Saints go Marching in'.

JR Ralph Casimir with Louis Gardier, Dr Herbert Severin, RC Martin and Casimir Morancie marched at the head of the procession keeping time with the band. Many of their followers waved the flags of red, black and green and were greeted by a roar of approval. 'Freedom...' they sang out lustily, 'Britons, never, never, shall be slaves!' It was a glorious day, the sun beaming down upon them as they celebrated 86 years since the Emancipation Bill had been actioned and 82 years since the end of enforced apprenticeship.

On the eve of Emancipation, those who governed the island had feared that once the island's 14,175 slaves were freed that there would be drunkenness and disorder. However, in true Dominican fashion, many simply went to Mass in thanksgiving.[121] It is also to be remembered that at the end of the period of enforced apprenticeships,

GRAND VARIETY ENTERTAINMENT.

UNDER THE AUSPICIES OF
The Roseau Branch of The U.N.I.A. and A.C.L.
Monday 2nd Aug. 1920, at The Liberty Hall.

—:0:—

PROGRAMME.

1. Tableau "The Call of the Hour."

CHARACTERS:

Marcus Garvey........................Mr. J. R. Roberts
Capt. Cockburn ....Mr. S. Stephen
Miss H. Vinton Davis................Mrs. Agnes Benjamin
Standard Bearer.....................Mr. B. O. Michell
   Comprising also of:—3 Nurses, 1 Medical Surgeon 1 Soldier,
   2 Sailors and Bugler.

2. Selection ....Orchestra
3. The Pantry Ghost Play, in 1 Act.

CHARACTERS:

The Pantry Ghost (known as Johnny)...Master P. Charles
Mary Ellen } Servants...............{ Miss M. Stephen Miss
Sarah Jane } ....{ M Casimir
Thimothy Pillpower, a Doctor's Boy....Mr S. Peter
Billy Butterscotch, a Grocer's Boy....Mr. J. H. Elwin
4. Song : "Let me live my life for you"..Mr. Marcus Adams
5. Chorus : "Go the Other Way"... ....Ladies
6. Recitation—"The African Banner"....Five Boys
7. Song..........................Mr. J. R. Casimir
8. Congo Act. Representing the African
   Customs—Miss M Casimir M's Una Jolly Miss Ethel Dow Miss
   Elorie Edwards, Mrs. Maria Casimir. Mrs. A. Benjamin,
   Mr. J. R. Casimir, Master B. Casimir.
9. Song "That's what God made moth-
   ers for"........................Mr. J. H Elwin
10. Magic Performance ....Prof. Roberts
11. Song ....Mr. S. Peter
12. Selection ....Orchestra

INTERMISSION FIFTEEN MINUTES.

1. Recitation 'Spelling of Marcus Garvey' Master P. Charles
2. Song..............................Mr. P. F. James
3. Monologue... ....Mr. L. A. Piveteau
4. Chorus—"Merrily the Phylis Wheat-
   ley will go"..................Children
5. Dosing the Doctor—Play in 1 Act.

CHARACTERS:

Pen Greedy—A Patient.............Mr. Clarence John
Bob Squills—A Doctor............Mr. J. Stephen
6. Recitation.......................Miss Olga Charles
7. Chorus—Wait till you get them up in
   the Air Boys :...............Men
8. Magic Performance...............Prof. Roberts
9. Song: Mamma, do not weep..Mother...Mrs. Agnes Benjamin
   Children..Miss M. Casimir and Miss
   Thelma Simon
10. Song.............................Mr. T. Skerritt
11. Recruiting Sergeant (Comic)

CHARACTERS:

Sergt. Dasher.......................Mr. Skinner Reid
Timothy } Country Yokels......{ Mr. J. Stephen
Johny Bamboo } ....{ Mr. B. O. Mitchell

DOXOLOGY.

The programme for the Grand Variety Entertainment held during the Emancipation celebrations of 1920 featuring the Casimir family in song and dance roles.

55

in 1838, the slaves had started 'full free' with nothing. Days before, John Longley, Dominica's lieutenant governor, read out a declaration: 'The Houses in which you live and the Grounds which you have planted, are not yours.' He assured them that if they continued to work as they had for their Master, he would allow them to remain in 'his House, and plant your Provisions on his Grounds. This is what I advise you to do; what I know the Queen, would wish you to do'.[122] The Master would, of course, receive compensation for the loss of his slaves. The slave owners of Dominica received a total of £275,547.[123]

Throwing back determined shoulders, the marchers continued towards their destination: St Gerard's Hall, set back from the road behind the Cathedral, was a solid building and had been the place of worship for Catholics before the central part of the cathedral had been completed and was now used for meetings and official ceremonies. It was here that the Emancipation Rally was to be held. That day it was surrounded by a great press of people; some were already in the main room of the building, while others clamoured to enter. The air was filled with aromas from the coal pots of the vendors, delicacies such as the fishy *ackra lamouie*,[124] honey-sweet plantain fries, spicy *boudin noir*[125] and *callaloo*.[126]

Soon the hall, gaily decorated with flags and bunting, was packed. The programme began at 10.30am with a prayer and, again, singing of the hymn 'From Greenland's Icy Mountains'. Seated on the platform were Francis Gardier, president general; Joseph Steber, the chairperson for the day; Ralph Casimir, general secretary; Herbert Severin, president of the Roseau Division, Casimir Morancie; JR Roberts and RC Martin, and other UNIA officials. Gardier welcomed everyone to the rally and introduced Steber as the chair. He remarked that he had been chosen because of the ready cooperation and advice that Steber had freely given to him and the officers of the Association. He believed that in order to make progress the movement needed support from all sections of the community. That would not be easy to come by.

Joseph Steber thanked the officers, spoke of the honour of being invited to chair the function and his pleasure at being able to serve the organisation. He was disappointed that, except for Martin, the 'gran bourg' to whom many invitations had been extended had decided not to attend. Steber pointed out that those who found themselves in more fortunate financial and social circumstances were ashamed to identify themselves with these important celebrations and preferred to distance themselves from the leaders of the Association whom they had described as 'irresponsible boys'. He believed that as a member of the race whose emancipation was being celebrated it was an honour to be present. Steber also reflected on the importance of the Thanksgiving Service and reminded his audience of the past horrors of slavery. He cited some examples of cruelty which had been related to him by a former slave when he was a young overseer. It was freedom from atrocities and cruelty of the kind described that the descendants of the slaves were celebrating on that day. Steber himself was proud to be in their company and to observe the 'thoroughness of their behaviour'. The next to speak was Severin who spoke about the legacy of slavery, gave a report on Marcus Garvey and the activities of the UNIA in the Roseau Division.

Ralph Casimir in his speech surveyed the condition of the race from slavery to the present. He spoke of the history of slavery in the West Indies during which Negroes had been so harshly treated in the name of Christianisation. Despite 'freedom' from slavery in the West Indies and the United States, he said Negroes did not enjoy freedom in any real sense as they were denied the very essence of liberty and were still 'political serfs' denied a voice in their own government. The only recourse he saw was to follow the leadership of Marcus Garvey. 'We have been taught the old lesson,' he said, '"Britons shall nevermore be slaves", but certainly in a sense we Britons of the dark race are not a free people. Not being free in the land of other races we should rightly claim Africa for our home.'[127] He continued by saying that all should rally to Garvey's call. 'This is the race which he is fighting for and asking us to join. Negroes were not cowards either in France, Flanders or Mesopotamia. We should not shrink from the present fight for possession of our own Motherland.'[128] He ended with a rallying call for all present to join the Association in the knowledge that there were others gathered this very day in New York and other West Indian islands discussing liberty and democracy for the Negro race.

RC Martin, the only 'gran bourg' merchant to attend, congratulated the Association on its achievement in the short time since its inauguration in Dominica and declared that it was the first time in the history of Dominica that such a large gathering of its African people had come together and it had taken place through their own will and organisation. It proved their ability to organise and direct their own lives. He praised the New Negroes, who were engaged in self-improvement and spoke of the noble work of the UNIA Divisions on the island. They were certain to meet with opposition but should not be daunted. ES Jones, the secretary of the Pointe Michel Division, delivered a speech concerning liberty and the meaning of true freedom. He was followed by HJ Elwin whose words were equally well received.

In his closing remarks, Steber observed that the black people of Dominica deserved all the benefits enjoyed by the white races including access to heaven. One day, they would all be given the right to vote.

The speeches were received with enthusiastic cheers with the audience giving tumultuous applause at the end of each delivery. Then everyone joined the UNIA members in a rendition of 'Africa Our Home' once the speeches were over. They declared St Gerard's Hall to be their own Liberty Hall and declared three cheers for His Majesty the King, Steber, Marcus Garvey, the UNIA and the local organisations. Then all stood for the 'National Anthem'. Only then did the vendors begin to serve the refreshments from their coal pots.

During that day, Masses and celebrations were also held by rural UNIA branches on the island: in Grand Bay, Marigot, Wesley and Soufriere. Records show that the enthusiastic audience in Soufriere was addressed by Gerald Grell, Z Joseph, Peter Léger,[129] Thomas Etienne, Miss F Maynes, RA Seraphin, the secretary, and WJ Seraphin, the president of the Division. They, too, thanked the Lord for the day and spoke of a future when Dominicans would make real progress and be treated as equal citizens in their own land.

That evening, back in Roseau, crowds again crammed into Liberty Hall for a variety show of orchestral music, songs, drama, farces, recitation and magic. All performed by UNIA members. *The Congo Act* was a dramatic performance in which a variety of African customs were showcased. The audience enjoyed *The Pantry Ghost* which was presented as a comical farce. Songs included 'Go The Other Way', which was sung in parts by the lady members of the Roseau Division, 'Up In The Air', 'Lia, Lia', 'The Black Star Line' and 'Merrily The Phyllis Wheatley Will Go'. The enthusiastic audience kept shouting encore at the end of each performance. Roberts, the chairman of the Roseau Division, entertained the crowd with his skills as a magician. The performance ended with a tableau showcasing *Africa The Land of Opportunity*.

The *Dominica Guardian* reported that it had been 'a most enjoyable evening'. The entertainment was such a success that it was repeated the following evening to a packed audience, some who came for a second viewing.

The following year celebrations took a very different turn. As we have seen, Ralph Casimir had left Dominica in June 1921 to sail to Trinidad in order to advise and support both burgeoning and established UNIA Divisions and did not return to Dominica until mid-August. He was not present for the Emancipation celebrations that year and there is no official record that the local Roseau Division marked the occasion. However, the *Dominica Guardian* ran advertisements for celebrations to be held in the village of Soufriere on 1 August 1921. The organising committee for the event were 'gentlemen of the place':[130] Gerald Grell, Thomas P Etienne, Peter Léger (these three had been involved in the previous year's celebrations), magistrate Parry Bellot, TC Etienne, Percy Olivaccé,[131] schoolmaster Zephaniah Jones, with the support of Joseph Steber.

A few days later, an extensive account entitled 'Emancipation Day Fete At Soufriere' was carried in the *Dominica Guardian*. The village was gaily decorated with bunting and arches of flowers and foliage. Special arrangements had been made to carry large parties, including a band, by boat from Roseau, Pointe Michel and Grand Bay. There was an air of excitement in the seaside village. Among the specially invited guests were the 'administrator, the Hon R Walter, Hon T Cools-Lartigue, CA Seignoret, Cecil EA Rawle, RW Royer, CG Phillip and many ladies.'[132] Had Casimir been present he would have noted that some of those who attended — all members of the establishment and the mulatto elite — had turned down invitations to attend the previous year's celebrations by the UNIA.

The Soufriere celebrations began with a high Mass. Visitors and residents crowded into the picturesque 18th-century Catholic church set in the Soufriere Bay. It had been fashioned from blocks of volcanic stone at its inception; then in the 1880s it was fitted with exquisite stained-glass windows and marble altars which were imported from France by Father Antoine Auguste Vergene. So crowded was the church, that many had to be satisfied with worshipping while standing at the doors and windows.

The service was followed by aquatic sports which included a double-scull race and a *pwi pwi* (raft) race; both took place in the bay with the onlookers cheering from the beach. Monetary prizes were awarded to the competitors. After this, the important visitors and the organising committee visited Olivaccé's home for a hearty lunch. Street vendors were on hand to provide for those who had not brought their picnic baskets.

The administrator had missed the earlier celebrations as the Treasury launch carrying his party broke down 'en route' and had to be towed by the Riviere family's launch. On arrival, the administrator's party were saluted in greeting as the band played 'God Save The King' accompanied by visitors and villagers singing and waving flags. This was followed by a welcome speech from Grell, who included some requests concerning the 'town's most pressing needs'.[133] The administrator responded at length and 'alluded to the day's celebrations in appropriate terms'.[134] The day continued punctuated with music from the band. The athletic races, which had been held back until the administrator's arrival, took place at 4pm. After recuperating at the Presbytery, he was on hand to give out the cash prizes and congratulate the winners. Steber thanked the sports committee and the community for their involvement and the administrator for his patronage and for his contribution to the funds for the day. He also thanked the 'kind hearted gentlemen of Roseau' and 'made a fitting allusion to the great event of Emancipation which they were celebrating that day'.[135] To end the day, more refreshments were had before the launches, canoes, horses and donkeys took the visitors home.

It is apparent that the Dominican elite found this type of celebration — one devoid of politics and one that did not confront them with uncomfortable truths — far more palatable than the event of the previous year. At a time when many burning issues remained, pertaining to education, health, housing, employment and standards of living, from Casimir's point of view the Soufriere celebrations had avoided the fundamental questions that needed to be asked about a society that denied most Dominicans political and economic autonomy.

Under British colonial law, the right to vote was based on wealth and land ownership. For more than a century after Emancipation, the majority in the Caribbean were subjected to the legislative whims of the upper classes and denied true representation in government. These were the issues that Ralph Casimir and the Dominica UNIA highlighted and called on for change. It was not until 1951 that Dominicans were granted universal adult suffrage.

5

Challenging Political Power

While Casimir's most intense activism — on behalf of the Garveyite movement — focused on those few years in the early 1920s, his involvement in Dominican politics lasted until the mid-1950s. His work was crucial in highlighting the plight of the poor and campaigning for reform of the legislature which, until 1936, consisted of four elected members, two nominated members and six officials. He opposed those in power, both the colonial and local elites.

Having been sacked by Rawle for his UNIA activities in 1920, Casimir briefly joined the teaching staff of the Roseau Boys' School in 1922. The school was housed in a former 18th-century munitions building on the sea front behind a wall in Newtown, just south of Roseau. However, his employment there was cut short by an eye accident. Rushing forward during one recess to intervene in a fight between some students, he was hit in the eye by a stone thrown by one of the boys. The injury resulted in partial blindness in one eye which affected his sight for the rest of his life.[136]

Casimir resigned from teaching at the end of the 1923 school year and got a job as a bookkeeper on the Canefield estate, owned by Andrew Green. Then, in April 1924, despite their previous disagreement, he re-joined Rawle's chambers as a legal clerk.[137] Rolle was in dire need of an efficient clerk and, by this point, Casimir had resigned from the UNIA and the movement had dissipated in Dominica. With that conflict of interest removed, Rawle was keen to re-employ him, knowing of Casimir's scrupulous attention to detail and efficiency.

The move back to working for Rawle enabled him to be at the heart of Dominica's politics for it was Rawle who, although opposed to Casimir's radical views, was a key campaigner for political and socio-economic reform in Dominica and the Caribbean region.

In 1927, the influential Dominica Taxpayers Reform Association (DTRA) was formed,[138] chaired by Rawle, with Casimir as its assistant secretary. What was to become a powerful body had been started by the mulatto and Negro elite to challenge the inequalities of the taxation system unchanged since Crown Colony rule had been imposed in 1898 when Dominicans had lost the right to vote in elections. Although there had been earlier taxation changes, introduced by Governor Viscount Gormaston in 1888, when a two per cent tax on property and earned income was imposed, there remained inequitable differences in which merchants and landowners escaped paying their share of the taxes.

One of Casimir's jobs with the DTRA was to travel around the island to organise its various branches outside Roseau. The DTRA's committee would later praise him for his organisational skills.

It was against a background of agitation for political and economic reform, not just in Dominica but throughout the region, that the DTRA with Rawle at the helm, organised the regionally important Dominica Conference (known as the West Indian Conference), which ran over six days from 28 October 1932. It was the first time that delegates from all over the English-speaking Caribbean had come together. Chaired by Rawle, Casimir was one of its two secretaries. Casimir's role would have been crucial to the smooth running of the conference. He would have had to be present and involved in every step, at the planning stage as well as overseeing the day-to-day running of the conference, including the registration of participants, taking of

Casimir family album

CEA Rawle, lawyer, Casimir's employer and at times his political adversary.

minutes, and recording all decisions and proposals. Following the conference, there would have been the task of drafting and distributing the conference report.

The opening and closing ceremonies were held at the St Gerard's Hall while the conference sessions took place in the large central room of the Union Club in Roseau, the club[139] for the elite mulatto members of Dominican society.[140]

The main aims of the conference were to consider the options for West Indian confederation and self-government; in effect, to chart the political development of the English-speaking Eastern Caribbean. Seventeen delegates attended: from Antigua, Barbados, Dominica,

Grenada, Montserrat, St Kitts, St Lucia, St Vincent and Trinidad. The delegates were idealistic and passionate in their vision for the region. 'Plans for the operation of a general government of the British West Indies were outlined, but there was a sharp divergence on how voting for the federal representatives should be conducted.'[141] While universal suffrage was proposed by AA Cipriani, who represented the Trinidad Working Men's Association, there were objections from the 'moderate, middle class'.[142] Eventually a compromise was reached and the conference agreed that the definition and nature of franchise would be left to the interpretation of each local legislature.[143] Delegates believed that an elected majority in the legislature of each island should be their main objective and that the islands have internal self-government.[144]

Later that year, the Closer Union Commission, appointed by Britain to look at the possibilities of integration among the region's British colonies, reported that they 'were impressed with "the spirit of earnest reasonableness" of the local political leaders.'[145] The commissioners, who described Dominica as one of the most political of the islands,[146] recommended a federation of the Leeward and Windward islands which would follow the pattern already established in the constitutions of the Windward Islands and Dominica. Unlike the Leeward islands, the electoral principal had been granted to them by Lord Irwin in 1922 and was established in their constitution.[147] The governor would not be attached to the administration of any one particular island but would be based in a central place, the favoured location being St Lucia. He would have oversight of all the islands by travelling to them fairly frequently and would be the sole communication between the islands and the Colonial Office.[148] The proposals for reform of the islands' constitutions were to be put before the various legislatures for discussion and consultation.

Meanwhile, Casimir continued working as a legal clerk and a

*The delegates to the famous West Indian Conference,
masterminded by CEA Rawle, in 1932. Casimir (back, far right)
was one of its two secretaries.*

bookbinder to support his growing family. He had married Thelma
Giraud in 1927 and by this time had five children.[149] He was also on
the list of jurors made up of men from all over the island who could
be called to sit on the jury during criminal trials. This could be an
onerous and time-consuming task and for jurors living in Roseau it
was unpaid. This proved a problem for wage-earners with families to
feed who lost income while attending court. Casimir, too, felt the
hardship of undertaking jury service and, in 1933, he presented a
petition, on behalf of 33 jurors, to the acting administrator of
Dominica, Thomas Baynes, to be forwarded to the governor of the
Leeward Islands, Thomas St Johnson. The petition asked that an
ordinance passed by the legislature in 1927 allowing payment to jurors
living outside Roseau be extended to jurors from Roseau. Casimir
claimed that the petitioners were 'men of humble occupation who
have to undergo much hardship' to earn a livelihood, that many had
large families and 'our means of livelihood (is) barely enough to
provide ourselves with three meals a day'.[150]

The letter asked for a meeting to put their case. Baynes agreed to meet with a delegation of three: Casimir, MJ St Rose and Evarard J Giraud[151] but ultimately the petitioners' request for remuneration was denied. The only concession was the introduction of free medical certificates for jurors from government medical officers when unable to attend sessions because of illness. Following this decision, Casimir wrote to PI Boyd, the registrar of the Supreme Court, requesting that his name be removed from the list of jurors: 'I have a wife and five children to maintain and cannot conscientiously serve on the Jury.'[152] (Casimir's name reappears on the jurors' list for 1944.)

In the wake of the 1932 conference and the Closer Union Commission, pressure for legislative reform continued to build. In March 1934, a conference of unofficial delegates from the Windward and Leeward islands was held in St Lucia to discuss the Commission's proposals. Following objections from Grenadian delegates in particular, it was decided that it was not practical to continue with the initial proposal for federation.[153] However, there would be changes to the composition of the legislatures and all the islands would apply a combination of nomination and election to their membership. The exact detail of franchise would be decided at a local level, but it was generally agreed that universal adult franchise could not be put in place until the standard of education had improved.

It is evident from an article in the *Dominica Tribune* of 10 August 1935 that the DTRA had already received details of what was likely to be put forward by the Closer Union Commission in the new arrangements for representation at the legislature and confederation. The main issues centred on representation and the proposed composition of the Dominica legislature. Rawle, the DTRA chairman, shared his concerns: 'With only four executives and two Crown nominees [there is] the temptation to the electorate to discriminate against a certain section of the community, and the equal temptation to the government to discriminate in favour of that particular section. We want a Legislature drawn from or representative of every class in the community and capable of serving the interests of the Presidency as a whole, without any reference to any narrow conceptions of black and white.'[154]

Casimir would have been in favour of this proposal for it is evident from his earliest writings that he believed in representative government, and that Dominicans should be in charge of their own destiny. The case for greater representation of local members on the Legislative Council was put to the Closer Union Commission and this resulted in an increase: from 1936, it would include the governor, three ex-officio members (attorney general, treasurer, and administrator), two nominated members and five elected members (an increase of one).

However, relationships between Casimir and Rawle continued to be fraught. While Rawle was a dynamic lawyer with keen political instincts, these were more reformist than radical, and in 1935, Casimir and Rawle clashed again. In this instance, Casimir and 15 others from a range of backgrounds, including the well-to-do Allison Boyd, signed a memorandum that was sent to the Legislative Council accusing the officers of the DTRA, which included Rawle, its chairman, of neglecting their duties. It also stated that 'the objects of the Association have not been served... That the unofficial members[155] of the Legislative Council of Dominica have betrayed the trust reposed in them by the People of Dominica.' It called upon the DTRA officers, who in this case were also unofficial members of the Legislative Council to resign, to acknowledge that the Association did not support the policy of the unofficial members and to appoint a committee before which the Association's policy could be put for discussion. The signatories also requested that the motions contained within the memorandum be presented to the administrator.

Rawle struck back through the columns of the *Dominica Tribune,* which he co-owned and edited from 1924-37. On 7 September 1935, in an editorial headlined 'Puerile and Unwarranted Attack on Unofficial Members of the Legislative Council', he attacked the contents and signatories of the memorandum which had been sent to the Legislative Council. The editorial described the memorandum as 'a pitiable exhibition of inanity'. It pointed to an 'absence of responsible signatures' and claimed that it had been devised through the 'conceit and vanity of misguided and disgruntled youth'. It dismissed the claims against the officers and accused the signatories of a lack of gratitude towards the 'gentlemen who have unselfishly and at considerable cost to themselves devoted many years of service to the public'.[156]

Casimir responded in a characteristically robust and detailed way attacking the officers of the DTRA on a range of grounds. In a unpublished letter to the *Dominica Tribune,*[157] he pointed to irregularities around 'non-financial members' and accused Rawle and the acting secretary of the DTRA of not dealing with the letter of the signatories according to the rules of the Association. Refuting the claims made in the editorial, he went on to cite rules which had been broken, including the Association's neglect in holding the necessary general meetings for the election of officers. He accused two unnamed official members of the Roseau Town Council and DTRA of misleading the people of Dominica, of authorising unnecessary expenditure and of appointing friends to certain positions. He also maintained that they had reneged on the promises for a covered public market in Roseau and complained of the neglect in the upkeep of common facilities regarding the condition of the streets, and the provision of lighting and water.[158]

As well as setting out complaints against the DTRA, the memorandum had raised an additional matter. It was that a request be sent to the British government asking that it give support to the

Ethiopian government to counter the imminent invasion of Ethiopia by Italy. Rawle's editorial of 7 September in the *Dominica Tribune* was not sympathetic to this request: reading it as a call for a public meeting, the editorial declared that this would risk 'stirring up racial animosities in so excitable a population' and 'should not, in our opinion, be lightly disregarded or unnecessarily inclined.'[159]

Casimir's position was that it was not enough to express sympathy for Ethiopia. Through his reach and contacts, Casimir would have been aware of the events taking place in Africa, in particular, Mussolini's resolve to take Ethiopia. By early 1935, a build-up to a full-blown Italo-Ethiopian War was becoming inevitable. This stoked support for Ethiopia all over the Caribbean: it is 'hard to over-estimate the impact of the war on the popular consciousness of the West Indies.'[160] Even before the invasion on 6 October 1935, the Colonial Office received a flood of petitions from UNIA Divisions all over the

Casimir was deeply committed to Haile Selassie, emperor of Ethiopia, and his country's fight against the Italians in the 1930s.

Caribbean demanding that Britain take a stand against the Italians and do more to protect Ethiopia. There was intense frustration in the face of what was interpreted as European complacency.

Cecilia A Green asserts that the *Dominica Tribune* 'was devoted to presenting and publicising the political agendas and achievements of Rawle's small political group and defending it against all challengers'.[161] She goes on to cite three examples to illustrate that elite group's perspectives on race and class.[162] This chimes with Casimir's assertion recorded in his reports to the UNIA[163] that the political leaders on the island were fearful of the challenge to the status quo. Birth and family name have always been used as currency and shortcuts to indicate class and privilege. In the 1930s, the surnames which counted would have been those associated with the ruling elite and merchant class. Gradations of colour also carried weight. What was known as the 'mulatto ascendency' had become well established in the wake of the 'Brown Privilege Bill' passed in 1831, three years before Emancipation, allowing political and social equality to all free non-whites.[164]

During the 1930s, those stirrings of nationalism and a reshaping of politics played out differently within the elite, the petit bourgeoisie and the peasantry in Dominica. The coloured elite, who distanced themselves from the majority black population, were striving for status and power within the existing colonial system. Thus it was important for the leaders of the DTRA and the Roseau Town Council to be viewed as legitimate players and to distance themselves from those, such as Casimir, who challenged the existing power structure and who came from a different class.

The language used in the editorial to describe those who had signed the memorandum clearly indicated that these young men were neither from an 'acceptable' class nor were they responsible citizens — they were merely 'hotheads' or communists who could not be taken seriously. This is ironic given Rawle's comments at the August meeting

JB Charles, with his daughter Eugenia (later prime minister of Dominica) and his wife Josephine. Charles, an affluent merchant, was a quiet supporter of Casimir and the UNIA.

of the DTRA, referred to earlier in this chapter,[165] that the legislature should be drawn 'from every class'.

The use of the *Dominica Tribune* to manipulate political outcomes was evident again during the elections to the Roseau Town Council held in October 1935. Electoral franchise was determined by wealth and property. By this time Casimir owned his own house and had an annual income of over £25.00. This meant that not only was he able to vote in local elections but he was also eligible to stand as a candidate for the Roseau Council elections. This he duly did. Of the nine candidates, five were standing for re-election: Cecil Rawle, Ralph Nicholls, Edmund Tavernier, PO Winston, and LA Piveteau. There was also an independent candidate, Oliver Didier, and three opposing candidates: JB Charles, JRR Casimir and FLC Royer.

A leading article in the *Dominica Tribune* of 2 October 1935 set out to enlighten the voters of the worthiness of some of those seeking election.[166] The work and leadership of Rawle, Nicholls and Tavernier were remarked on, and much was made of Winston and Didier who were described as 'promising young merchants', although Piveteau was accused of 'seeming to run with the hare and hunt with the hounds'. On the other hand, voters were warned against supporting the three opposition candidates who were deemed as having nothing to offer the electorate. The opposition's manifesto beginning 'Ladies and Gentlemen, we are faced today with the question, Are we fit to demand the right to govern our own affairs?' was ridiculed; and they were scorned for their lack of prowess in sport and their inability to be 'eloquent and cultured public speakers'. The latter comment was a clear assault on the education, class, and background of the candidates in question.

Come the election, the recommendations of the *Dominica Tribune* were upheld, and Rawle, Nicholls, Tavernier, Didier, and Winston were duly elected. The paper published an account of the votes cast: Nicholls 120; Rawle 112; Tavernier 103; Didier 91; Winston 83; Charles 49; Casimir 40; Piveteau 34 and Royer 20. In the speeches that followed the count, Rawle reminded those assembled that he had refuted the attacks made on himself and other Council members. Both he and Nicholls asserted that they were 'clean' politicians. Tavernier, Didier and Winston promised to do their utmost for the town. JB Charles said that he had been a candidate in order that 'Town Councillors would be kept on the alert'. He also pointed out that their manifesto had been deliberately misinterpreted. The three remaining candidates thanked those who had voted for them and Casimir confirmed that he hoped to fight the next election.[167]

Like Casimir, JB Charles came from humble beginnings. Like Casimir, he, too, had left school at 14. A self-made man who started off his working life as a stonemason, he saved enough money to buy his first piece of land in 1901 and built his first house a few years later. Like Casimir, he regarded himself as a Pan-Africanist and encouraged his children to read Booker T Washington's *Up from Slavery*. He had served on the Roseau Town Board in 1923 and had been an elected member of the legislature from 1928 and in 1931. He was a man of means and had also been a delegate at the 1932 West Indian Conference. Despite this record, the editor of the *Tribune* had not hesitated to ridicule his candidacy when he stood in opposition and aligned himself with Casimir.

During this period of the mid-1930s, Casimir continued to work in solidarity with Ethiopia. Through his UNIA links, Casimir had set up the Ethiopian Defence Fund and took charge of collecting money for the cause. He was in correspondence with Dr Malaku Bayen, then personal envoy to Emperor Haile Selassie, who set up the Ethiopian World Federation with other Ethiopian exiles in 1937 and invited Casimir to join the organisation.[168] He subscribed to the weekly *New Times and Ethiopia News* in which some of his poems were published and was also in regular correspondence with its founder and editor Sylvia Pankhurst.[169] Pankhurst regarded the Italian invasion of Ethiopia as a violation of the principles of the League of Nations and began a campaign to pressurise the British public and government to take steps to support Ethiopia. She believed that fascism should be stopped and wrote in *The Times*, 'If the Fascist Government is allowed by the rest of the world to succeed in its aggression against Abyssinia, this will be but the prelude to yet more terrible aggression.'[170] She tirelessly raised funds and was to later become a close confidante and adviser to Emperor Haile Selassie. She moved to Ethiopia in 1956 and lived out her life there.

Meanwhile, Rawle, on behalf of the legislature of Dominica, dispatched a resolution from the colony of Dominica supporting the British denunciation of the Italian invasion of Ethiopia, but went to great lengths to distance himself from those factions he described as 'communist agitators' and 'rabid racialists'. He was at pains to dispute the claims being made by the Pan-Africanists of the racial nature of the war by claiming that 'the Italian is not white and the Abyssinian[171] not Negro'.[172] Rawle's pro-imperialist stance, despite his avowed commitment to Dominican self-government, bore fruit when he was appointed to the post of attorney general of the Leeward Islands in 1937 and moved to Antigua where he died in 1940.

As we have seen, Rawle and Casimir had a complicated relationship: they were divided by class and education but held each other in mutual respect. Rawle valued Casimir's skills as a clerk — he found him efficient, conscientious, hard-working and meticulous in his recording and record keeping. Casimir valued the opportunities that opened up for him as Rawle's employee and respected his efforts to ensure that the people of the colony should have a measure of self-determination in their government. Yet he refused to allow his employment to compromise his principles and political beliefs.

Rawle may have admired Casimir's passion but he found his willingness to stand up to the status quo embarrassing and annoying. Rawle's status allowed him to operate at a different level within the elite mulatto and white leaders of Dominica. In contrast, as a self-educated black man, Casimir did not have the cultural capital or economic resources of those who regarded themselves as his betters. Casimir's struggle was one for equality; he spoke for those of his class and experience.

Even so, Casimir wrote a congratulatory letter to Rawle on his appointment in the Leeward Islands: 'I sincerely congratulate you on your appointment[173] as attorney general of the Leeward Islands and trust that you will so conduct yourself and execute the duties of high office without fear or favour or ill-will, that both friend and foe will be compelled to respect you and you will be an inspiration to the sons and daughters of Dominica.' In his response, Rawle thanked Casimir sincerely for his kind message and added, 'It is indeed a source of deep gratification to me to know that I shall assume the duties of this office with the good wishes of my friends.'[174] And when Casimir had married Thelma Giraud, Rawle wrote to Casimir and his new wife a letter of congratulation.[175]

During the years following the demise of UNIA Division 85, Casimir had remained an active member and supporter of the UNIA. He regularly contributed articles about Dominica and poems to the *Negro World* until its publication ceased in 1933 (Casimir's interest in and dedication to poetry will be explored in chapter 6), and he continued to follow the work and life of Marcus Garvey with profound interest.

By then Garvey was living in Jamaica, where he was elected as a town councillor to the Allman Town division of Kingston in 1929 and set up the People's Political Party, Jamaica's first political party in the same year. However Garvey found himself harried on all sides as he was denied the right to speak in the places he visited. He spoke out against the judiciary and was imprisoned for three months for contempt of court. He was released on bond and later tried and convicted of seditious libel with a six-month jail sentence. He appealed against this and won. He contested a seat on the Legislature in 1930 but lost to the Honourable Seymour-Seymour, a white Jamaican. Finally, in 1935, having found it difficult to stay afloat financially and struggling to make ends meet, he sailed to England where he continued campaigning to raise consciousness about the issues and injustices which affected black lives.[176]

Despite his anti-establishment views, Casimir was against Communism, preferring to describe himself as an African Nationalist. In a letter to the *Negro Worker*[177] in 1936, he wrote, 'While there is certainly a certain amount of good in Communism there is also a great deal of harm therein, and I personally am not in agreement with most of what Communism teaches. Frankly, I think Communism is a menace to the Negro. It... cannot help the Negro one iota... I am an

African Nationalist.'[178] He withdrew his support from the magazine and said he was no longer willing to circulate it in Dominica. He believed that it had become a vehicle for communist ideas. In a further communication with its editor, Casimir used the example of Soviet Russia and its complicity with Mussolini by supplying his army with oil during the Italo-Ethiopian War to explain his objection to Communism.[179] 'No white nation takes the Negro seriously!'[180]

There was one further event that stimulated the political awakening of Dominicans: Marcus Garvey's tour to the Eastern Caribbean in 1937. On his way to the Caribbean, he had travelled from London to Canada to attend its annual UNIA Conference. There, speaking in Nova Scotia, Garvey said that in order to take control of one's destiny, black people must 'emancipate ourselves from mental slavery…, none but ourselves can free our minds' — words immortalised in the lyrics of Bob Marley's 'Redemption Song'. Garvey then embarked from Halifax aboard the *Lady Nelson* on a lecture tour throughout the Caribbean. As Garvey made his way through the island chain, he was, according to newspaper reports, met with huge crowds and great applause. The main message of his lectures was that only through self-reliance and political determination could black people expect to achieve economic and political success.

Before arriving in Dominica, Garvey had visited and lectured in Barbados, St Vincent, Grenada, Trinidad, British Guiana (Guyana) and St Lucia. There had been some debate around allowing him to land in Trinidad where there was unrest among oilfield workers but that was lifted on the proviso he refrained from political speeches.

When wishing to arrange his visit to Dominica, Marcus Garvey wrote to a Mr Cruickshank who passed the information on to Casimir and left the planning in his hands. Robert Hill, a leading authority on Garvey and the UNIA, suggests that Garvey had not written to Casimir because he was trying to ensure that he would be met by a person of greater influence and prestige.[181] If that was the case, JB Charles would have been a better choice. It is possible that Garvey no longer had access to the files that would have contained the correspondence with Dominica (it was now 12 years since the Division had disbanded). It is also possible that he was given the contact by someone who had links with Cruickshank. I can find no reference to Cruickshank in documents of the time.

So it was Ralph Casimir who took charge of making the arrangements for Garvey's visit to Dominica on 30 October 1937. He organised the venue and informed the police that he had made a booking at the Coronation Hall.[182] However it was JB Charles, a discreet supporter of the UNIA, who paid the expenses and made donations to Ethiopia's fight against the Italian invasion. Casimir regarded Charles as an ally. Eugenia Charles remembered attending the occasion at the Coronation Hall, with her father. She also claimed to have attended other meetings at which Casimir spoke.[183]

Ralph Casimir must have been excited to receive the man who he had so admired and who had been his inspiration in his youth. He would have believed it to be a great honour to introduce Marcus Garvey to the audience at Coronation Hall. Curiously little is known about the visit except two newspaper comments on his speech. Casimir himself did not report on it except in his response to an article in the *Chronicle*. In other islands, lunches and dinners were laid on in Garvey's honour and it is probable that this would have been replicated in Dominica. The visit, however, was brief and the *Lady Nelson* is likely to have sailed on to its next destination that evening, on its way to St Kitts, Nevis and Montserrat.

Garvey's visit was reported in the 6 November editions of both the *Dominica Chronicle* and the *Dominica Tribune*. The *Chronicle* remarked that Garvey 'received a tumultuous welcome when he landed by a crowd which surged around him enthusiastically'.[184] However, the brief article was generally negative in tone reporting that it was disappointed with Garvey's philosophy of life, as, it surmised, he did not believe in charity, humility or altruism. His only belief was in 'ruthless ambition' and that he spoke of God in a patronising way. He had stated that the only perfect man was Jesus Christ but had not referred to his divinity and that was bordering on heresy.[185] However, it did acknowledge that 'The well-known Negro organiser certainly has a powerful personality as the way in which he held the crowd plainly showed'.[186]

Casimir was displeased with the *Chronicle*'s coverage and fired back a critique published in its edition of 17 November. 'You stated that Garvey does not believe in charity. How untrue! Mr Garvey denounced those who, rather than work honestly for a living, rather than endeavour to improve their educational, social, and financial positions, choose to be ever subservient to others... You stated that Mr Garvey believes in ruthless ambition but you gave no explanation to support your statement. What you call ruthless ambition is an ambition of the Negro to rise to the level of his inconsiderate "masters" in intelligence, industry, commerce, government, etc... You may think it impossible, but civilisation flowed down, not up, the Nile!... You failed to give an explanation of what you call the "patronising way" Mr Garvey treated God... Do you disagree that God does not want certain things?... Mr Garvey's philosophy of Life is not surprising. He was speaking to a Negro audience. He knows the Negro needs and aspirations.'[187]

The *Tribune*'s report was more positive commenting on the crowded hall and carrying a summary of Garvey's hour-and-a-half long speech on the subject of 'The Power of Thought'.[188] The report stated that Garvey had urged his audience to accept the importance of thinking for themselves, of owning their own minds. He claimed that letting others think for them only resulted in being used to the advantage of those who would prefer to have the ordinary negro 'sewn up in a bag'. He stressed the importance of self-study in order to identify one's capabilities and abilities in order to put these to use and achieve one's capabilities. Garvey reminded his audience that while there was merit in the mental and spiritual influence of God, his wonderful creations and dominion over life and death, it was men who had used their minds to create scientific and technological development. 'When we refuse to think for ourselves we prostitute the Intelligence of God.' There was no reason that a Dominican could not rise to the accomplishments of Shakespeare or Napoleon. This and more could be achieved only by 'cutting the bag of ignorance and darkness in which they had been placed by more fortunate people who could capitalise from this'.[189]

This would be Garvey's last tour of the Caribbean and, wherever he spoke, he proved a charismatic speaker. Indeed, his speeches are remembered and now studied throughout the Caribbean. In a speech made by Prime Minister Timothy Harris of St Kitts-Nevis in 2020, he made reference to Garvey's iconic speech to the islanders in 1937, quoting him when he said: 'Make St Kitts your Garden of Eden. If you don't do it then other men will do it for you... Watch your steps. If there is natural wealth around, somebody is coming after it... Your country can be no greater than yourselves... Your St Kitts will be no greater than your minds... If there is progress, it will be because of your minds'.[190]

Marcus Garvey died in London on 10 January 1940 following two strokes. Affected by the death of the man whose vision he had embraced, Casimir commemorated him in his poem 'Marcus Garvey – Dead'.

> And nations raved and plotted
> But Marcus fought unbowed,

> And e'en behind prison bars
> There Garvey was uncowed.
> I drank from Afric's fountain
> Of pride of race a lot
> By following his teachings
> And inspiration got.[191]

Casimir was eventually elected to the Roseau Town Council in the 1940s (having stood unsuccessfully in 1933 and 1935) and served two terms. Elections were a lively affair and fiercely contested by the candidates and their supporters. Each candidate was represented by a symbol chosen by himself. Casimir's symbol was a hand, signifying the power of the written word and the ability to get things done. He was an ardent councillor and attempted to use this role to address issues which affected the people of Roseau. Typically, he found himself in opposition to the views and decisions of some of his colleagues. In July 1945, for example, he threatened to resign over what he regarded as broken promises around both increased taxation and an increase in water rates. He stated, 'It is inopportune at present when the water service is inadequate and unsatisfactory, when there is such a fearful chasm between employer and employee, and when poverty is rife.'[192]

Casimir was dedicated to using his position on the Council to improve the living conditions of the poorest Dominicans. He was aware that many were living in insanitary and slum conditions and he became involved in a campaign to rehouse and support those who had settled in the coastal area across the Roseau River, north of the town centre. After Emancipation, landless former slaves had no choice but to settle illegally where they could find unoccupied land. Invariably this was most often within the King's Three Chains (the strip of land of 66 yards inland from the sea, once used by the Crown). Sales of land were restricted to those who could pay above a set minimum price and only in parcels of land of at least 40 acres; this put the poor at an inevitable disadvantage.[193]

Owing to the plantation economic structure imposed by the British from 1763,[194] Dominica had been, to its detriment, a largely one-industry island, first producing sugar then limes followed by cocoa, vanilla and, much more recently, bananas. Production was disrupted by disease and war as well as by cheaper and more lucrative markets. In 1928, it was clear that this could no longer continue, and diversification was necessary. However there appeared to be no drive or overview from the colonial powers or from the local legislature to organise and oversee a mixed agriculture. As late 'as the 1930s the great majority of the population earned no wages and depended solely on their own food crops'.[195]

The landless carved out a living as had their maroon forebears, on borrowed land, raising their *ti kais* and shanty 'lean-tos' wherever they could. As the Moyne Commission, set up in 1938 to investigate the reasons for unrest in a number of the British Caribbean islands, put it: 'Of all the British West Indian Islands... Dominica presents the most striking contrast between the great poverty of a large proportion of the population, particularly in Roseau, the capital, and the beauty and fertility of the island'.[196]

In May 1946, the government purchased both the Goodwill estate and Pottersville, also known as Balahoo Town,[197] the latter situated to the north of Roseau, at the mouth of the Roseau River. However, progress to carry out the plans for rebuilding and allocation or sale of lots was painfully slow. As a member of the Roseau Town Council, Casimir continued to agitate on behalf of the people of Pottersville, in particular. Several residents who were living on rented lots, had, prior to the government purchase, made an agreement with the landlord to buy the lots they occupied. Many had already paid the required surveyors' fees. In February 1947, Casimir organised and submitted a petition, signed by more than 60 people, on behalf of the people of Pottersville to the governor and commander-in-chief of the Windward Islands, Sir Arthur Francis Grimble, asking for this issue to be resolved and that a resolution regarding the matter, passed at the Roseau Town Council four months previously, be acted upon. The petition was signed by Casimir (elected member, Roseau Town Council), Ed McD Tavernier (merchant and druggist), VL Ducreay (proprietor, shopkeeper, wine merchant), MW Joseph (photo artist), Z Josephs (teacher), and Lucy Rock (proprietress and seamstress).[198]

A response was received via the administrator's office assuring the signatories of his sympathy for the 'temporary inconvenience' but stating that no steps could be taken until the survey of the Goodwill Estate and the Pottersville area took place. They were waiting, they said, for the arrival of newly appointed qualified surveyors from the United Kingdom.[199]

In the correspondence between Casimir and the colonial government over 18 months, he regularly raised the issues that beset the residents of Pottersville. He wrote to Edwin Arrowsmith, the administrator, that sanitary conditions were becoming progressively worse, pointing out that part of the area had become 'a mere swamp or quagmire'.[200] He highlighted the anomalies around rent collection and harassment by bailiffs and that the promised arrangements for purchase of lots were yet to be realised. He asserted that 'while plans are being lingeringly drawn, the tenants' building materials are rotting and their burdens are becoming unbearable, financially and physically'.[201]

Following the findings of the Moyne Commission in 1945, the Slum Clearance and Housing Ordinance was passed in 1946, the same year as the purchase of the Goodwill estate. In 1951, the Roseau Council published plans for the Second Supplementary Goodwill Scheme. Notice was being given that lots were available at the cost of £1 a year, payable in advance. The stated purpose of this scheme was to provide adequate housing sites for those who were not able to comply with the building requirements which had been set out in the First Supplementary Goodwill Scheme. It further confirmed that this was a slum clearance strategy 'specifically planned for the relief of conditions in the slum areas of Roseau'.[202]

Casimir had begun to highlight the issues of housing, slum clearance and proposed a solution several years before action was taken. The wheels of the colony and its agents, the legislature and the Roseau Town Council, were bureaucratic and sluggish in taking up this challenge. In 1953, those in charge were still discussing how a scheme to support the most disadvantaged could go forward. The administrator set up a working group to investigate an aided self-help housing project modelled on a scheme operated in Antigua.[203]

Representatives spoke to the Roseau Council at the end of 1952. The scheme propounded many of the ideas which Casimir had first suggested five years earlier: affordable housing, built to an agreed standard with financial support and sold to 'tenants thereof of humble means on a hire purchase system'.[204] A pilot scheme was finally discussed by the Council in 1954[205] but little was achieved.

In 1955, Casimir stood as an independent candidate for the Legislative Council in a by-election for the Roseau North constituency, which included Pottersville — and Goodwill. Opposing him was Allison Boyd, a radio engineer, who 20 years earlier had supported Casimir in his criticism of the DTRA. Casimir's programme focused on improved housing. His aim was 'to eradicate the slums of Pottersville' to give the highest priority to the provision of houses to the poorest; provide vocational education and opportunities for youth to train as tradesmen and craftsmen; to agitate for a large modern school in the Balahoo Town area; and to provide those in need with family allowances.[206] It was an ambitious manifesto also featuring the promotion of tourism, improvements in the road system and better agricultural training.

For Casmir, the election campaign was fraught and at times frightening. His attempts to outline his manifesto and his advocacy on behalf of the poor of Balahoo Town and the need for proper housing was disrupted at one meeting by a small group in the crowd, and Casimir had to abandon his speech. As well as heckling, stink bombs were thrown, and, as the *Dominica Chronicle* reported in its editorial 'What Is It Then' of 9 March 1955, the audience was 'stupefied with odours of various kinds... so the beautiful programme which had been outlined for the welfare of the people of Pottersville housing scheme and family allowances... was hushed!' Shocked by this display, the editor asked whether the agitators were 'being misled, fooled, deceived and deluded into a most false impression of what Government is supposed to be, or what the duties of a representative are?' It began with reference to a sitting member of the Council who despite 'the dire and atrocious lack of housing' was not prepared to make this part of his agenda. It contrasted this with 'Mr Casimir's programme which conforms to all that is to be expected of government.'[207]

Roseau was a small place where most people would be known by name or reputation. Yet the *Chronicle*, despite its sympathetic tone, failed to name them. However, it did suggest that the 'destructive activities' were 'all to satisfy the mind of one seeking to take revenge over others for all his sufferings'. It also advised that anyone who 'needed medical attention for diseases of the mind' should be banned from standing as a candidate for the Legislative Council for at least three years after diagnosis. It was known that Boyd had suffered from mental health issues during the 1950s.

In an open letter to all voters, in the *Dominica Chronicle* of 19 March, Casimir stressed that although Boyd had held a seat on the Council for the previous six months, he had done nothing to benefit the people and had failed to carry out promises made in his previous manifesto. He also stated that Boyd had refused to sit on any of the council committees. Casimir accused Boyd and his gang of trying to disturb his public meetings and of perpetrating falsehoods.[208]

My aunt Clara remembers her father was once attacked in the street during the campaign, in the early hours of one morning, on his way to the 5am Mass he regularly attended. He was violently beaten and had to spend a few days in bed. Octavia (Dolly) described this as a 'horrible time'. She said that the family was very fearful and that at night Casimir would sleep with a gun under his pillow.[209]

Casimir lost the election by a resounding 669 votes to 161. He was defeated in what he described as a campaign characterised by 'mud-slinging, deliberate lies, slander and persecution'.[210] It is to be noted that Frank Baron,[211] who had previously won the Roseau South seat and was to become one of Dominica's pre-eminent politicians, was one of the first to congratulate the victor. After this unpleasant experience, his close friends, Samuel J Lewis, a headmaster, and Elias Nassief, a Lebanese businessman and entrepreneur, advised him to stay out of the political arena.

It would be many years before building began in Goodwill and the rehabilitation scheme for Pottersville took place. Casimir continued to express his views and submit his poetry in local papers, and, although he remained committed to change and took a lively interest in politics, he had by then largely bowed out of active political life. However, he believed that he had played an important part in agitating for change and that part of his vision for Balahoo Town had been realised.

6
The Grandfather
of Dominican Literature

In the literary history of Dominica, Ralph Casimir numbers among a generation of writers who were born on this small and little-known island at the turn of the 20th century. They include Jean Rhys, Phyllis Shand Allfrey, and Daniel Thaly. Unlike Casimir, all three were from affluent and well-connected families. It is unsurprising then that their careers followed different paths; even so, just as he did, they remained 'profoundly marked by the social history of their home island at a specific moment in time'. [212] While it is unlikely that Rhys would have known Casimir as she left the island some years before his arrival in Roseau from St Joseph, we do know that. in his later years, Allfrey became a friend and confidante, and that, much earlier, Thaly, who wrote in French, had contributed to the first anthologies of Dominican verse, compiled and edited by Casimir.

Ralph Casimir was a determined man who believed that against all odds ordinary Dominicans could be writers and poets. His efforts in this were recognised and appreciated both in Dominica, in the wider Caribbean and in the US. It is in this respect that Alick Lazare, Dominican writer and a former leading civil servant, referred to Casimir as 'the grandfather of Dominican literature'. Alwin Bully, former chief cultural officer of Dominica, has also described him to me as 'the pioneer of Dominican literature'. With a passion for the printed word, and books, in particular, he wrote poetry almost compulsively; he was an editor, a journalist, a book seller, a book collector, and critic. In one of his poems, 'My Books', he exalts in his pleasure of reading, saying that he feels like a 'duke — while I devour the contents of my books'.[213]

Casimir's schooling would have exposed him to the works of the English poets. Francis Palgrave's *Golden Treasury*, and Nelson's *Royal Readers* would have been commonly available in West Indian schools of the time. It was a key pedagogical device for school students to be expected to memorise and recite poetry from such textbooks. In this way, pupils were also introduced to Shakespeare, Milton and the British Romantic poets. For Casimir, this fostered a deep appreciation of the English poetic canon, its forms and conventions.

Although his formal education may have ended at an early age, he took every opportunity open to him to further his own education. Through self-education, he became a knowledgeable man. He also had some mentors to guide him. Among them was Randall H Lockhart, a relative of ARC Lockhart. Randall Lockhart was educated both in Martinique and in England. He went on to study law, was called to the Bar in 1922 and subsequently returned to Dominica to practise law. In a letter to Casimir in 1924 he writes: 'I did not lend you the Longfellow; I made you a present of it. I think that every man of taste should have something of a library, and I have no doubt that you have already got together a few books. I am afraid the Longfellow is not too presentable, but it is worthwhile your having until you get a better edition.'[214]

Lockhart offers some Shakespeare plays of which he has duplicates to 'enrich (his) poetical feeling', Bunyan's *Pilgrim's Progress* and two anthologies from among the best known English poets. He also offers to go through some of Casimir's poems and give some help with the rhymes as he thinks that Casimir needs guidance with that aspect of his work. 'I will go through them and work the imperfect rhymes.' He then goes on to discuss the importance of prose and to recommend 'a course of reading following up the development of the English novel'. Included in the letter are a list of authors and publications. The five-page letter ends with some advice on a source concerning parody which he believes might be helpful.[215]

No doubt Casimir found such guidance useful, and the tone of the letter suggests that the two men must have spent time together discussing literature and their love of poetry. He would also have been appreciative of the gift of the books to begin to build his own library.

The first evidence that we have of him as an independent writer is in 1919, in an impassioned political piece entitled 'Race Prejudice', in which he asks: 'White men, give your reasons, if any and if you can, for being so hateful of the Negro Race?'[216] From this point he not only writes letters and submits articles to local and regional newspapers but as we have seen becomes a regular contributor to Marcus Garvey's *Negro World*. It is likely that he was inspired to try his hand at poetry through the influence of this newspaper.

The *Negro World* was much more than just an organ for the rallying cry of the UNIA, the paper published poems, short stories, book reviews, and articles about works of literature. It was also a forum for literary critics: Zora Neale Hurston, author and anthropologist; Arthur Schomburg, historian and archivist; Alain Locke, philosopher and activist were among the well-known figures who wrote for it regularly. It was also a space in which aspiring writers, such as Casimir, from the African diaspora, could publish their work. The *Negro World* ran literary competitions, and readers were encouraged to send in essays, short stories and poems. The judges, Garvey himself and William Ferris, a Yale graduate and author, who was literary editor of the newspaper, were insistent on the importance of literary excellence when awarding prizes.[217]

This plethora of black writers of the time, through the medium of the *Negro World*, helped to usher in the Harlem Renaissance of the 1920s with an unparalleled promotion of African-conscious literary activity. Garvey defined the aesthetic of this literary offensive in his essay on 'African Fundamentalism': 'The time has come for the Negro to forget and cast behind him his hero worship and adoration of other races, and to start out immediately to create and emulate heroes of his own. We must canonise our own saints, create our own martyrs, and elevate to positions of fame and honour black men and women who have made their distinct contributions to our racial history... We must inspire a literature and promulgate a doctrine of our own without any apologies to the powers that be. The right is ours and God's. Let contrary sentiment and cross opinions go to the winds.'[218]

In this manifesto, Garvey established the philosophical foundations of his work in which the first principle was rooted in the dignity of Africans and New World Africans. This was founded on his belief in God, and that people of African descent as expressions of the divine could 'out of our own creative genius we make ourselves what we want to be.'

Casimir's writings for the *Negro World* would have placed him at the hub of black literary life at the time despite his geographical isolation. Indeed, Tony Martin, the Trinidadian-born scholar of African studies who died in 2013, described him as being one of the most prolific *Negro World* poets.[219]

Casimir produced and published poetry for more than seven decades, from 1919 to 1995, both locally and internationally. Sometimes writing under the pseudonym of Civis Africanus (Citizen of Africa), he published nine anthologies[220] of his own work, and also edited and contributed to four anthologies of the writing of Dominican poets. The first record of a published poem was an acrostic in the *Negro World* in 1921 when he was 23.

> Wake up, ye sleeping Negroes
> On to victory!
> Raise thy voices fearlessly:
> Liberty for Africa and Africans,
> Down with traitors, oppressors all![221]

His work regularly appeared in Dominican newspapers, but he was also published in the US publications, *Crisis*, *The Crusader* and the *Philadelphia Courier*. At least one of his poems, 'To the Africans at Home',[222] was published in the *Gold Coast Leader*.

Casimir's poetry was often political and was described as militant by both Martin[223] and Lizabeth Paravasini-Gebert,[224] the biographer of Phyllis Shand Allfrey. In 'Dominica and her Afric Sons', for example, published in 1922, he accuses Britain of exploiting black soldiers and their regiments during the first world war only to disregard them in the wake of victory. He charges the colonisers with duplicity and urges Dominicans to embrace their heritage as 'offsprings of historic Africa'. He implores them to resist any efforts by 'prejudiced Englishmen' to treat them as 'inferior men'.[225]

In 'Forgotten Heroes' (1923), he attacks the claim that the first world war was fought to ensure freedom and self-determination for all British subjects. By appropriating John McCrae's well-known poem 'In Flanders Field', he presents an alternative perspective of reality to 'transform the storied battlefield from a symbol of British heroism to a site of West Indian valour in the face of adversity'.[226]

> In Flanders Field where poppies grow
> They were surrounded, as we know
> By Belgian and English 'foe'
> While German guns them down did mow
> In Flanders Field where poppies blow

Casimir's contempt is not only for the British government but also for the state of government in Dominica. In a poem written in 1974, more than 50 years later, 'Whither Dominica?', he laments: 'political bosses tell people to make / sacrifices when… bosses fatten their own purse'. In another of his poems, 'The Forces of Evil' (1978), the year that Dominica became an independent nation, Casimir describes the state as 'a rudderless ship' and fears for the move to independence 'In a poor, crippled nation'.

Much of Casimir's poetry reflects his Pan-African beliefs and preoccupations. The poems are at times rallying calls, such as 'Black Man Listen' (1972), designed to scold for 'wasting monies thrown in our laps', to instruct as well as to raise awareness of the achievements of the black figures of history and also to instil racial pride. 'How do you study history?/ … get inspiration from/ Imhotep … revered as god of medicine/ Euclid the mathematician'.

Some of his poems were praise songs for those whom he admired, both in Dominica and further afield. We can see this in 'O Loving Sage' (1923), where he praised WH Ferris of the *Negro World*: 'Thy precious words so bold, so true/ A noble spirit in us imbue'. In a poem dedicated to Joseph Hilton Steber, editor of the *Dominica Guardian*, who had given support to the UNIA, Casimir urges, 'Put not aside your pen, my countryman… You are guardian, you are leader'.[227]

As well as reflecting his values and ideas, Casimir's poetry demonstrates the scope of his reading and his keen interest in world events. 'Hats off to Bellegarde' (1931) is an acrostic poem inspired by a speech by Dantés Bellegarde, a leading Haitian academic, historian and diplomat, to the League of Nations in 1931. Casimir hails him as 'Afric's spokesman, a brilliant star'. He was an advocate for the ending of United States' occupation of Haiti. In his speech, generally regarded as a work of oratorical and diplomatic brilliance, he said that American foreign policy was a danger to world peace. Casimir also corresponded with Bellegarde and sent him a copy of *Poesy Four*. In his response, Bellegarde is complimentary about the anthology and offers to put him in touch with the director of the National Library in Port-au-Prince.

'Battling Siki' claiming 'A new victory has been won for all our race' was written in honour of Louis Mbarick Phal, popularly known as 'Battling Siki', to celebrate this French-Senegalese boxer's success against the French and European light heavyweight champion Georges Carpentier in 1922.

Black leaders and icons such as Nelson Mandela, Martin Luther King, Marcus Garvey and key members of the UNIA, Angela Davis, and the early poet Phyllis Wheatley were honoured by Casimir; and he even found time to praise Winston Churchill.

More intimately, he also used poetry to celebrate the lives of friends and loved ones. His poem 'Farewell', written in memory of his mother after her death in 1944, carries a simplicity and poignancy:

> No more, alas
> I see your loving face
> No more I feel your motherly embrace

Many years later, in 1987, he wrote 'Adieu Mon Cher Ami', to lament the passing of his dear friend Elias Nassief, a well-known local businessman, and to celebrate his life. Several poems in both *Freedom Poems* (1985) and *Hurricane & Other Poems* (1995) express his support for and admiration of Prime Minister Dame Eugenia Charles and to honour her achievements.

> The Ship of State speed her full sail,
> Riding o'er the waves through the gale.
> Steer her steady off reef and shoal
> Till we safely reach our goal.[228]

Louis Mbarick Phal 'Battling Siki', the world light-heavy-weight boxing champion of 1922, was one of many black figures who were praised in Casimir's poetry.

These, however, were not the only subjects which inspired Casimir's poetry. On publication of *A Little Kiss and Other Poems* in 1968, Allfrey remarked when promoting the anthology in her newspaper, the *Star*,[229] that readers would find the subjects quite different from Casimir's usual poetry. In general, the poems are flirtatious, and play with the ideas of love and heartache. His most risqué musing is to lament that there 'was no kissing'.[230]

> Not much ease, through jalousies,
> With heaving heart and longing
> Just to hug her, just to kiss her[231]

Casimir was a family man, he used poetry to express delight in a new baby: 'Two little eyes of innocence/ Two little eyes that shine like stars/.../ The loving eyes of baby mine'.[232]

Whereas, in the main, Casimir's poems are written in standard English, in his most playful lyrics Casimir uses the local English-based Creole, as in this poem:

> W'y you's hidin' an' hidin' so,
> Peepin' an' peepin' thoo de do'?
> Ah! Me see you, gal, don' run,
> You yeye shinin' lak de sun[233]

The topics of his poems in English Creole were either describing market days, schoolchildren playing or love interests. In this, Casimir was ahead of his time as he was writing in the 1920s when the only form of writing acceptable in the British West Indian colonies was Standard English. It was two decades later that Louise Bennett (1919-2006), commonly known as Miss Lou, a celebrated Jamaican poet and folklorist, began to speak and write poetry in Jamaican patois in the belief that the people's language mattered and should be celebrated; her ideas met with controversy. Later, Edward Kamau Brathwaite (1930-2020), a major voice in the Caribbean literary canon, described the Creole languages of the Caribbean as 'Nation Language' and gave them legitimacy.

Ralph Casimir also wrote in the French-based Kwéyòl (though he would have called the language Patois) of Dominica. This would have been spoken widely in his village and may well have been his first language. This was not the accepted language of the literate classes and its use was repressed and forbidden in schools. He uses this particularly in the poems which celebrate Dominica's carnival and culture. Code switching is prevalent in the everyday speech of Dominicans and even those who are not fluent Kwéyòl speakers will use its phrases in their speech to express a depth of emotion.

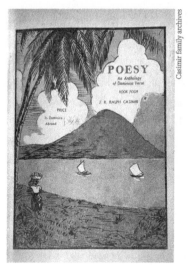

*The cover of Poesy Four (1948), one of four anthologies of
Dominican poetry compiled and edited by Casimir.*

Nous sav tan Canaval c'est tan jewté

Toutes moune venir Canaval celebré

Venir compere, enous chanter

Venir, coumere, enous danser[234]

This is one of Casimir's last poems, written in 1991, by which time
he had lost his sight. He recited it to his friend and priest Father Jolly
who wrote down the verses.

A recurring theme in all his poetry is the celebration and assertion
of his deep Catholic faith. He uses his poetry to pay homage to God
and his religion. Some of his poems such as 'Credo' and 'Agnus Dei'
are explorations of the meaning of Catholic prayer. As Phyllis Shand
Allfrey, describing him in a dedication as 'dear friend and fellow
Dominican poet', says of his poetry in her introduction to *Black Man,
Listen And Other Poems*, 'These are Christian poems. They are patriotic

poems of a man with a conscience. They are Victorian in that they use the verse form and terminology of Victorian and Early Edwardian times… lyric, assonance, blank verse, sonnet, scansion and so forth… They are the poems of a kind, loving and tough man.'[235]

Casimir is thought to have founded Dominica's first literary society[236] in 1921. Known as the UNIA Literary Club, it held monthly meetings,[237] and, modelled on the UNIA literary clubs then flourishing in Jamaica, became a forum for debate and discussion where members were encouraged to read both the work of other writers and to write their own stories and poems.[238]

In the wake of the society's founding came the island's first published anthologies of poetry. Between 1943 and 1948, Casimir compiled and edited four volumes of poetry written by Dominicans, including Daniel Thaly. These were titled *Poesy An Anthology of Dominica Verse Book One*; *Poesy An Anthology of Dominica Verse Book Two*; *Poesy An Anthology of Dominica Verse Book Three* and *Poesy An Anthology of*

Daniel Thaly, a Dominican poet writing in French, was a contributor to Casimir's Poesy anthologies.

Dominica Verse Book Four. Contributors to the four anthologies were, apart from Casimir himself, largely but not exclusively drawn from educators in Dominica. There were also three women poets, but the most distinguished of Casimir's contributors were Vivian Dalrymple, later better known as Edward Scobie, and Daniel Thaly. (For details of the contributors to Casimir's anthologies see Appendix 1.)

Casimir himself contributed to all four books. His poems in the first anthology, such as 'Africa Arise' and 'To the Africans at Home', are testaments to his Pan Africanism.

> They can imprison the body but not the will
> The spirit of liberty they cannot kill:
> Like an invisible wind it rushes on
> To destroy the slavish work that men have done.
> They scorn and they kill; gird your loins
> And pay them back in their own coins.[239]

He also included dedications to George Washington Carver in 'Hail, Wizard of Tuskegee': 'With grace to lead / Thy race indeed' and to ARC Lockhart, the man who had founded the *Dominica Guardian* and led the Representative Government Association:

> Quiet in Death's untiring soundless reign
> The silver tongue; and we in silence bow.
> O Dominica, how great thy loss! Thou
> Shalt never urge his earthly fights again.[240]

Daniel Thaly, whose poetry is still lauded and studied in France, was most certainly the most renowned of the contributors to the *Poesy* anthologies, and his poetry appears in *Poesy Three* and *Poesy Four*. Born in Roseau but educated in Martinique before going on to study

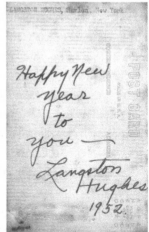

Langston Hughes, the leading writer and activist of the Harlem Renaissance, corresponded with Casimir, as in this greetings card for 1952.

medicine in Toulouse, Thaly was the son of Solange Bellot of Dominica and Dr Hilaire Thaly of Martinique. He practised medicine in Dominica from 1905 to 1938, worked in Martinique as an archivist during the second world war, before returning to Dominica in 1945 where he died in 1950. He wrote exclusively in French and, in his lifetime, published nine volumes of poetry. His work was 'precise in form, and meticulous in its descriptions of exotic landscapes. Thaly's poems were characterised by evocative images of Dominica and Martinique...'[241] His poem 'Clair De Lune A Minuit', for example, idealises Roseau:

> *Roseau la nuit semble une ville*
> *Des mille et une nuits*
> *Aux parfums des jardins de l'île*
> *Se mêlent ceux des fruits*[242]

Vivian Dalrymple, who contributed two poems in *Poesy Two*, had left Dominica to join the Royal Air Force and served as a flight lieutenant in Bomber Command during the second world war. He later became known as Edward Scobie, working in England as a journalist and, in 1972, as the author of *Black Britannia*, the first book about the African presence in Britain. In a letter to Casimir, Scobie wrote from England: 'Actually I would like you to send me two copies of the Poesy - Book II in which my poems appeared. Enclosed you will find a postal order of five shillings to cover the cost and the postage.'[243]

It was not long before news of these pioneering anthologies spread beyond Dominica. In New York, the Harlem Renaissance poet Langston Hughes wrote in a letter to Casimir in 1952 that he had added the anthologies to his personal collection of West Indian poetry. Hughes also informed the Poetry League of Jamaica of their existence. In a letter from Wycliffe S Bennett, secretary of the Poetry League of Jamaica, to Casimir, dated 7 September 1950, Bennett writes: 'I've just received a letter from Mr Langston Hughes in New York, in which he very kindly told us about your recent anthology of Dominican verse... We shall be grateful, therefore, if you will be so good as to send us as early as possible a copy of "Poesy".'[244] In a further letter from Bennett, he writes, 'It is a real pleasure to learn that Dominica is evolving its own literature. We realise too that you are the godfather of all this activity. Thank you for so promptly sending us the four editions of POESY.'[245]

Casimir was also in regular correspondence with Thomas LG Oxley, who established the Colored Poetic League of the World and invited Casimir to become a member.[246] He gave Oxley much-needed support in compiling *An Encyclopedia of Negro Anthology*. Oxley sought help claiming that this would be 'a work that has never before been attempted in America. This work will consist of two volumes; the one, the Foreign Negro Bards; the other, the American Negro Bards.'[247]

As we have seen, Casimir's own influences were the classical poetry of Milton, Pope, Keats, Tennyson and Wordsworth. In *Scriptum*,[248] an anthology of some of his own writing, he gives an insight into his ideas about poetic verse in a brief article, 'Poets and their Critics', written in 1955.[249] He criticises Thomas Gray's 'Elegy Written in a Country Churchyard', which he refers to as 'a classic museum of unnatural poeticised atrocities'. He also gives Dylan Thomas short shrift and comments that 'Perhaps when Dylan Thomas has learned to differentiate between substance and shadow he will add lustre to our language.'[250]

Casimir believed that any poetry writing should be kept to strict classical poetic forms and that any departure from that should be distrusted. His own writing adhered to the prevalent characteristics of Victorian poetry with its focus on sensory elements as seen in his more lyrical verses 'Blessed Isle, such as O Dominica/ Verdant land of sparkling water',[251] and 'The slender branches of allamandas … danced blissfully in the breeze/ that kissed my tender cheeks'.[252]

His use of verbal embellishment is apparent in a poem to celebrate the Grenadian politician TA Marryshow,[253] in which Casimir addresses him as 'Grand Old Man of the Western Isles'; 'Daring the storms of hate, unbowed';[254] while in his farewell poem to his wife, Thelma, who died in 1989, he begins it with 'Phoebus with the clouds plays hide and seek'.[255]

His final anthology, *Hurricane & Other Poems*, published in 1995, one year before his death at the age of 97, is dedicated to all Dominicans. He rejoices in the beauty of the island 'Siffleurs whistle their sweetest lay/ Beneath the sun's effulgent rays' while raising concerns for the future. 'Where is progress? Strife and squalor'. Other poems in the collection are laden with guidance for significant figures of the day: to Marie Davis Pierre, Speaker of the House of Assembly,

Casimir family album

Best Wishes for
a Merry Christmas
and a year
of Happy Days

Christmas Greetings card from Ralph Casimir, date unknown.

he advises, 'Fear not the ravings of the pests/ The lying tongues, the dirty threats'. He uses the poem 'Give me music', dedicated to the musician Lemuel Christian, to celebrate and honour Dominica's own musicians alongside the classical greats. The poem, 'Hurricane', was first published in the *Star* after Hurricane David in 1979. While the storm is a howl of anguish and destruction making the people 'fearful, shocked, hungry, disconsolate', in contrast it leaves an unforgettable silence in nature.

> Where are the dove, the hummingbird, the titine?
> Where are the cricket, the lizard, the crapaud?
> There is no chirping, no cooing, no croaking[256]

As previously mentioned, Ralph Casimir used poetry to commemorate people who had held significance in his life and to eulogise them. 'A Friend' was dedicated to Sylvia Pankhurst in praise of her services to Ethiopia 'N'er you falter, e'er unafraid/When will our debts to you be paid?'[257] In 'Farewell Dear Spouse', he speaks of his own loss, acknowledges his own failings within his marriage and celebrates Thelma's patience and compassion, 'She pardoned me for offences committed/ She forgave me for services omitted'.[258] In his 80th year, looking back on his life he wrote:

> When comes my time for eternal sleep
> Lay me down in the City of the Dead
> Beneath the smiling flamboyant trees[259]

Casimir loved poetry, especially what he regarded as that which used the 'perfect' word. In his introduction to *Poesy: An Anthology of Dominican Verse Book Four*, he wrote: 'To me, the writing of poetry is a work of love, and I think whatever time is spent in reading and/ or writing of poetry is well spent.'[260]

Most of Casimir's writing tackled problems that were of social and political concern. He was idealistic, concerned with issues of truth, love, justice and the corruption of those in authority. He believed in the power of words and the power of poetry to express ideas, to enhance life, to celebrate and to bring about change in the country he loved. He dedicated his writing to that purpose.

7

Trials
and Triumphs

Casimir maintained strong and supportive relationships with his immediate and extended family. He also had a rich network of friends and acquaintances both in Dominica and beyond connected with all aspects of his long and dedicated life.

Casimir's contact with his mother remained close throughout his young adulthood.[261] She was still living in Roseau in 1931, but some time after this she and Meredith emigrated to neighbouring Antigua, taking Meredith's young daughter, Enid, with them. We do not know why the two women moved there but they must have believed that Antigua offered better prospects. Affectionate letters to Casimir from his mother indicate that Maria made a living by selling fruit sent to her by barrel from Dominica. In one letter, she asks him to 'send a barrel of grafted oranges and provisions'.[262] Selling agricultural produce was one of the few ways that women could make an independent living at the time.

However life in Antigua was not easy. Meredith became ill and Maria wrote to Casimir for help with medical expenses. She asks him to speak to his father on her behalf and that of Meredith, Dudley Casimir's 'only one lawful daughter'. She wrote, 'I beg you kindly let pride aside and be humble for my sake... you are poor and have so many children and a wife to support so you cannot help me.'[263] Casimir was not on speaking terms with his father; he was a proud man and his mother knew that he would dislike having to turn to him for financial support even though it was not for himself. Many years later, my father Rupert told me that his father had not forgiven Dudley's infidelity and refused to recognise his half-brother, Diego.

We know that Meredith was hospitalised and had an operation; but some months later, in October 1933, she died, in Antigua, aged 29. In a letter to Ralph and Hubert after Meredith's death, Maria expresses concern about providing for her granddaughter whom she will now have to raise.[264] She hopes that the child's father will be of help. The eventual solution was for Enid to return to Dominica where she was raised by her paternal grandmother.[265]

Some time later Maria moved to Trinidad where Hubert joined her. There, Maria sold books, and once again Casimir helped out by procuring books for her. In one letter, she discusses sales and asks for 100 copies of *MacDonald's Farmers Almanac* for 1945.[266] She was planning to return to Dominica in November and asked Casimir to give notice to her tenants to evacuate her house in Queen Mary Street. It was not to be. A week later, Casimir received a telegram announcing her passing; she had had a stroke. Maria would have been in her mid 60s at the time of her death. Detailed letters to Casimir from Hubert and from Casimir's godson, John E Benjamin,[267] describe the circumstances of her death and funeral. They express their profound sadness and dismay. Both wrote of the support they had received from the Dominican community in Port of Spain. In describing the funeral, Hubert wrote that it was well attended; he was satisfied that 'the priest prayed a lot over the body. The priest met the corpse from the hospital, just like a 2nd class at home'.[268] A few months after their mother's death, Hubert again wrote to Casimir from Trinidad informing him that the grave had been lit for All Saint's Day and of his plans to furnish it with a cross. He added that the funeral had cost £70.00 and mentioned a debt of £20.00 that their mother had incurred; he was hoping that Ralph would help him to make the payments.[269]

These letters say much about the family's position within their society at the time and how they struggled to eke out a living. Unemployment was high in the early 1930s and, in Dominica, this was exacerbated by the return of those who had emigrated to Curaçao to work in the oil fields and associated industries. Casimir may have had little money to spare but he was prudent with his spending, and was financially able to help his family. Both Maria and Hubert knew this.

While the marriage of Casimir's parents ended in separation, his own marriage lasted 62 years. In 1927, he married Thelma Giraud, daughter of John Louis Giraud[270] and his common-law wife, Lucy Nicholas. John Giraud's family were originally French emigres from Martinique, who considered themselves white, while Lucy had been

Casimir family album

Wedding day, with his bride Thelma Giraud,
February 1927.

a maid in the Giraud household. As well as Thelma, they had two sons, Cyril Tadimus and Michael Evelyn, who migrated to Cuba as young men. Thelma was brought up in her parents' household along with four of her paternal aunts, Louisa, Josephine, Rose and Emma. The women took a great interest in their brother's olive-skinned, mulatto offspring and endeavoured to instil their values in Thelma. These carried the full mores of a Victorian and European view of respectability, as well as colonial perceptions relating to skin colour and class. So, when Thelma married the dark-skinned Ralph Casimir, they voiced their disappointment.[271] Racial categories in the Caribbean formed a hierarchical continuum within which being of mixed race and therefore lighter-skinned often resulted in a more privileged status. In Dominica, wealth, power and privilege resided with the descendants of the estate-owning mulatto families.

Ralph and Thelma had 15 children; the eldest, my father, Rupert, was born in 1927; the youngest, Sylvia, in 1950. Three of the children did not survive beyond infancy while a daughter, Mathilda, passed away when she was 16. Mathilda, a favourite in the family, was a gentle and generous individual. She had been preparing to enter the convent for a religious life when she fell ill. It is not clear what caused her death, but it is known that she had had a high fever and was hallucinating. It is quite likely that she had pneumonia. During the early hours of one morning, clad only in a thin nightdress and barefooted, Mathilda ran from her home to the convent to pray with the nuns. She died the next day. Of the children who survived into adulthood were four sons: Rupert, Cecil, Garfield and Felix. They were followed by eight daughters: Octavia (known as Dolly), Cecilia (known as Flora), Thelma, Mathilda, Clara, Gloria, Elsa and Sylvia.

Respectability and the trappings of middle-class life were important to the Casimirs. Respectability was 'based on Eurocentric norms and values, embedded in class-colour systems of stratification and promoted by white churches, European marriage and a colonial educational system.[272] In Dominican society, to be regarded as part of the middle class it was vital to be labelled as being from 'a good family'. It was believed that this could be achieved through religion, education, honesty, humility and discipline.

Casimir was a Roman Catholic, a deeply religious man whose beliefs framed all aspects of his life. In his early years in St Joseph, he had been an altar server; on moving to Roseau he soon became a cantor at the cathedral and a member of the church choir. He served in this way for 60 years. Casimir celebrated his religion in his personal and social life. In Roseau, he was secretary and counsellor of St Gerard's Guild for many years. Founded by one of the Belgian Redemptorist priests, Father Bossuyt,[273] in 1909, the Guild held regular meetings and encouraged Catholic men to become involved in sports, music and entertainment. During his lifetime, Casimir was also secretary of the Holy Name Society of Roseau, a member of the Legion of Mary as well as of Catholic Action. His children also joined and took part in the activities of the various Church societies.

Many of the Catholic priests, both French and Belgian, serving on the island were close acquaintances of the family and would visit the household. Some Casimir praised in his poetry. Two priests, in particular, were his friends. Kelvin Felix was the first locally born Dominican priest to serve on the island, and became a cardinal in 2014; he was followed by Father Clement Jolly who was, like Casimir, 'gens St Joe' (born and raised in St Joseph). Casimir and Jolly shared many interests and were close friends. It was Father Jolly who led the Requiem High Mass at his funeral in March 1996 and delivered the eulogy.

Casimir used his writing to bear witness to his staunch belief in the doctrines of Catholicism. This is demonstrated by an editorial on Darwinism in the *Dominica Tribune* that set out to refute Darwin's

Religion was an important part of Casimir's life. Here he is (at the back, with arrow) with other members of the Catholic prayer group, Legion of Mary, Roseau

theory of evolution and support the position of the Bible and the Catholic Church. Written in 1927, he states, 'Darwinism is all balderdash' and champions the arguments put forward by 'the distinguished scientist, Professor Rudolph Virchow' and 'the eminent American theologian, Rev. MP Hill, SJ' by quoting from their writing.[274] He furthered his arguments in defence of what he interpreted as an attack by atheists and unbelievers on his Catholic beliefs and the Church in 'Whither Are We Drifting?'[275] Once more citing evidence from the arguments of opponents of Darwin's theory, he attacks in particular Fredrick Sterns Fadelle,[276] an influential Dominican of the time whom he describes as a dangerous free thinker. Irving André suggests that 'Casimir's defence of the Church was an implicit attack on the seeming pretentiousness of the coloured minority' and that 'championing of the Catholic Church was, therefore, as much a defence of the working population.'[277]

I believe that Ralph Casimir was deeply troubled by anything that

Father Jolly and Phyllis Shand Allfrey, writer and politician, were both friends of Casimir in his later years.

appeared to contradict his belief. In the Catholic Church he had found a haven where he could practise his faith, use his voice in the sacred rituals of his religion and engage in intellectual debates with the many priests that he met and who became part of the fabric of his life.

Thelma was also deeply spiritual but she was also a superstitious woman and was not averse to consulting women who could help her to get glimpses of the future and advice about the herbs and potions that would help to achieve the results she sought in health and other matters. Like many traditional Dominicans of her era, she was covering all her bases.

The celebration of and attendance at Mass was an integral part of the daily routine of the Casimir family. There was also an adherence to rituals such as prayers in the morning and at bedtime, saying the family rosary, observance of holy days and fasting during Lent. The family had their own pew in the middle aisle at the front of the cathedral. Highlights for the children were Christmas and Easter when they would have new clothes and special food. There was always a ham at Christmas, 'sweet sparkling Sorrel... feasting tasty callaloo... with Lime and Belfast Redcap'.[278]

All the Casimir children received a secondary education up to school-leaving certificate standard. Rupert, for example, was awarded a scholarship to attend the Dominica Grammar School, which had been established in 1893 and aimed to prepare boys for the Civil Service. The three younger boys attended the St Mary's Academy, a Catholic boys' school established by the Redemptorist Fathers in 1932. The Casimir daughters all attended the Convent High School founded by the Sisters of the Faithful Virgin, which first opened its doors in 1858. All three schools were well regarded. The children were encouraged to use the library and to spend evenings reading and completing homework tasks. Casimir was keen that his children should be well-educated and have the opportunities of further study that had been denied to him.

The family was governed by strict rules. Discipline was an important aspect of family life and transgressions were met with punishment including the use of a strap. Like many Dominican parents of the time, they believed in the biblical proverb 'He that spareth the rod hateth his son: but he that loveth him correcteth him betimes'.[279] As a devout Catholic at a time when the message from the pulpit was not one of 'Jesus loves you' and forgiveness, but rather one of retribution visited upon sinners, punishment was seen as a way of ensuring that one's children would be guided to lead lives which would help them avoid eternal damnation.

Success as parents was measured by their children's ability to sit still and listen, to be helpful and cooperative. They should also be 'seen and not heard'; while 'back chat' was a punishable offence. (My own childhood bore some of these features; I remember the intense frustration of not being allowed to explain myself on the grounds that any rejoinder was 'back chat'.) The qualities of obedience and submission to parental decisions were expected and valued.

In 1929, two years after their marriage, Ralph and Thelma Casimir bought their home, 60 Old Street, in Roseau from JC Wyke,[280] a friend and fellow member of the Roseau branch of the UNIA. They paid £145.00 for the 1,402.6sq ft lot. An initial payment of £90 was made in May 1929. The balance was paid periodically over the months that followed and completed in July 1930.

Domestically, it was a busy household. As Clara, Ralph and Thelma's fifth daughter, explained, 'My mother was so busy, all the time. She cooked, made clothes as well as the housework.' Although there was some help, everyone had chores which they were expected to complete on a daily basis. As a youth my father's chores included sweeping up and washing dishes. Clara remembers: 'We didn't have much fun! Even after I'd left school and was working, I had to spend my afternoon off at home ironing.'[281]

As the girls grew up it was ensured that they acquired the necessary skills for home making and independence. My eldest aunt, Octavia (Dolly), remembers being sent to sewing classes during her summer holidays. The girls were kept on a particularly tight rein. On leaving school or church, they had to come home directly. They were only allowed to visit acceptable homes. They could not take a leisurely stroll through the Botanic Gardens or along the Bayfront with friends. They were not allowed to go to dances or the cinema except to see a religious film recommended by the nuns. They were also forbidden from taking part in carnival frivolities. Despite these constraints, my aunts remember some jolly times when they were able to invite friends over. They played music and danced in their backyard.

Even after my aunt Clara had left school and was working as a cashier at Nassief's store in Roseau she had to adhere to these rules. It was around this time that she left home to lodge with her godmother as she found life at home too restrictive. This did not stop her mother from interfering through constant visits and attempts to continue to ensure that Clara's life was as controlled as before. Godparents were chosen with care and were often related to the family or extremely close friends. Becoming *nennen* (godmother) or *pawen* (godfather) to a child is regarded as a serious and lifelong commitment. My aunts believe that although their father held the purse strings, it was their mother who was the ruling force in the household and their lives.

In the Caribbean, it was not unusual for parents to be extremely over-protective of their daughters. Parents feared that they might either become romantically involved with the wrong type of man or become pregnant, bringing shame and disgrace on the family.

Casimir was a stern but caring father who spent a great deal of time in his study but would sit with their mother on the veranda for a while in the evenings. Perhaps as his family grew and he was under increasing pressure to make ends meet, he would have spent less time relating to his children. Even so, Rupert, the eldest of the family, affectionately recounts the many walks and excursions he took with his father and brothers and the visits they made to friends and family on a Sunday after Mass. Aunt Octavia also has fond memories of going with him on boat trips to Soufriere and Pointe Michel.

Clara migrated to England as a young woman, where she married. When her father discovered that her first husband was physically threatening her, he telephoned Scotland Yard from Dominica. He made a complaint and communicated his concern for the safety of his daughter and her child. This led to a visit from two police officers to her home to hear her side of the story and offer her the chance of taking out a restraining order against her ex-husband.

Despite her marriage to the Pan-Africanist Casimir with his firm belief in black pride, Thelma was imbued with the colourism prejudices of her aunts, and invariably fell out with her daughters

Thelma Casimir in the 1950s

because of their choice of men. Her main complaint was that they were too dark skinned to be suitable. She invariably saw success for her daughters linked with marrying into the lighter-skinned population. Her attitude created tensions within the family. After having given up one relationship because of her mother's objections, Octavia fell in love with a man who fitted none of her mother's criteria. This caused an irreparable rift. Octavia left home and lodged with a friend until her marriage to John Robinson in 1963. Her mother refused to attend her wedding and would not allow her sisters to attend either. The only close family present were my father and grandfather. My grandmother never spoke to my aunt again. Octavia left Dominica in the early 1960s with her husband who had joined the Royal Navy. She did not return to Dominica until 1989, a few months after her mother's death.[282]

These prejudices raise a number of questions for me. Did Thelma regret her marriage to the man who proudly described himself as a Negro? Did she believe that by marrying a man who was dark-skinned had curtailed her opportunities in life and circumscribed her socially? It also begs many questions about their intellectual relationship and how my grandfather combined and compromised this with his lifelong commitment to racial pride and celebration of his African heritage. How did he reconcile their lives with his thirst for knowledge and his burning desire to embrace a wider world? I can speculate that their strong and abiding Catholic faith held them together, their belief that whatever their difficulties, they were bound together for life. Thelma was always clear with her children that their father's work was to be respected. His study was his domain, a space in which he could engage in his intellectual pursuits undisturbed. Whatever the answers, whatever their differences, all such relationships are complicated.

In 'Farewell Dear Spouse', Casimir expresses his love for her:

> In life with me, sixty years and one,
> Battles fought, battles lost, battles won
>
> I thank you for your loving care
> I thank you Lord for a love so rare.
> Sleep, dear soul, your long, last sleep[283]

Ralph Casimir was a charming man and well respected in his community with many friends and acquaintances in Roseau and around the island.

One of Casimir's closest friends in Dominica was Elias Nassief, a businessman who had migrated to Dominica from Lebanon via Suriname in the 1930s. The two men may have seemed to many as an unlikely pairing, but Nassief had a strong humanitarian ethic and was well known for his acts of generosity to the needy. This would have chimed with Casimir. Introduced to each other by Casimir's old friend JC Wyke, they discovered that despite their differing backgrounds they had much in common. They were both religious men with a strong belief in family. Nassief also prized Casimir's understanding of the political workings of the local government and his knowledge of the law through his work as a legal clerk. Casimir became Nassief's trusted confidant and provided him with legal advice. It was Casimir who handled many of the transactions when Nassief began to sell off lots of the Belfast estate, some miles north of Roseau, and collected the monthly payments on Nassief's behalf.

The two men often travelled together to Nassief's Geneva estate in Grand Bay, in the south of the island. Geneva had originally belonged to the Lockhart family and is referred to as Coulibri in Jean Rhys's novel *Wide Sargasso Sea*. He was also a frequent visitor to Nassief's homes both in Roseau and Geneva. They enjoyed many companionable walks in an area close to Grand Bay known as Morpo with its superb views of Pointe Carib and the Martinique Channel. Casimir's staunch

*Businessman Elias Nassief, with his wife Marie,
was a close friend of Casimir.*

support, close companionship and camaraderie were recognised by the family who would affectionately refer to him as 'the acolyte'.

The friendship lasted until Elias Nassief's death in 1987. Casimir wrote an elegiac poem which was read at his funeral. The poem praised the public and the private man but also spoke of their friendship and of the fire which had destroyed Nassief's home on the Geneva estate. The 1975 disturbances which led to the attacks on Nassief's home and the Geneva estate had their roots in a history of overcrowding, high unemployment and frustration among the youth of Grand Bay. Locals had been used to unrestricted access to the land which covered more than 1,000 acres from the shore to the mountain tops and there were many squatter settlements. On purchasing the estate in 1949, Nassief evicted the squatters and cleared the land, planting mainly coconut trees for copra production. It is not surprising that these actions caused hostility and friction between the landowner and the residents. In the 1970s, in the new climate of raised consciousness and political awareness, these feelings resurfaced. In 1974, following a series of incidents over a period of a few months, trees were cut down, property was vandalised, and Molotov cocktails were thrown resulting in the destruction of the estate buildings. At the same time Nassief's store in Roseau was destroyed by arsonists. Eventually the estate was purchased by the government and subdivided into agricultural and housing lots for the people of Grand Bay.[284]

> I was with him in time of calm and gale
> When we escaped from Molotov Cocktail
> He was with me in joy and sorrow
> When thinking and hoping for the morrow
> I was with him in time of fire
> He was with me in stormy water[285]

Phyllis Shand Allfrey (1908-1986) also became a friend in the last decades of his life. Allfrey, a writer and a politician, was a white woman who had been born in Dominica and whose maternal family had lived in the West Indies for generations. She had travelled to the US and Britain in her early twenties and returned to Dominica in 1954 with a vision for political change. Joining forces with a trade union leader, Emanuel Loblack, a man whose roots were in the peasant class of Dominica, they together founded the Dominica Labour Party (DLP), the island's first mass political party. The party took power in a landslide victory in 1958, but internal political rivalries prompted her expulsion from the DLP in 1962. Like Casimir, she turned to the newly formed Dominica Freedom Party (DFP), despite it being dubbed the party of the 'gran bourg'.

Both Allfrey and Casimir were founding members of the DFP and remained political and literary allies until her death aged 78, in 1986. Casimir claimed in an interview with Janet Higbie, Eugenia Charles' biographer, that he had never been involved with the DLP and it is clear from poems written during the 1970s that Casimir had no love for the governing Labour Party. In 'Revolt' (1971), he wrote, 'My heart revolts/against "dirty gutter politics"/dissension lies, deceit/ bad government'. He questioned in 'Be Ye Warned' (1972), 'What matter if I am a different Party/ Why can't we work together/for the welfare of the State'. He describes the leaders as 'honourable despots' who 'rule like tyrants/ without compassion and foresight'.[286] He wrote of Premier Edward LeBlanc's retirement from government in 1974, in 'Adieu Capitaine': 'He's a reckless, poor skipper... Don't care a damn for the limping ship/hence no account of your stewardship'.[287] LeBlanc's DLP government was based on socialist ideals and its base would have been mainly in the working class. However it would appear that as time went on, with the influence of 'a circle of hangers-on seeking to benefit from the spin offs of political patronage',[288] the party's ideals were tarnished and there was little tolerance of criticism and overt opposition.

It is likely that Casimir was influenced by Allfrey's expulsion from the Labour Party in 1962 for publishing an editorial in the *Dominica Herald* which was critical of the DLP's tax levies. He saw a closer alignment with his views in the DFP; he knew its leader, Eugenia Charles, from having worked with her and he had a history with her father, JB Charles. Casimir said of JB that his politics were sound, 'He was very businesslike in his dealings... He wouldn't get into trickery, he was quite honest.'[289] Casimir stated that he became 'involved with the Freedom Party from the beginning because I wanted to do the right thing. I knew she [Eugenia Charles] would be successful. If you do the right thing, you succeed.'[290]

Allfrey's literary interests also drew the two together. Her published works include a novel, *The Orchid House* (1953), an anthology of short stories, *It Falls Into Place* (2004), and three anthologies of poetry: *Palm and Oak, Contrasts* and, posthumously, *Love for an Island* (2014). Among Ralph Casimir's books and papers gifted to the Roseau Library is a testament to their friendship. In Casimir's copy of *Palm and Oak*, Allfrey wrote: 'To Ralph Casimir. Fellow Dominican, fellow poet and gentle friend with the author's affection. Christmas Eve 1973'; and in *Contrasts*, she wrote: 'To my dear friend Ralph on his 80th birthday with love from another Dominican Poet'. Along with this dedication is the following poem:

> Gentleness of friends
> Gentleness of friends is the wine
> Milder than milk
> Sipped in full Summer
> Under an open sky[291]

After a visit to the Allfreys' home, Casimir sent them a poem titled 'Sweet Home (For Robert and Phyllis Allfrey)'. 'Thank you for being so courteous/Greeted by your charming smile/... with food and drink so generous'.[292]

Among one of Casimir's close associates was the Dominican journalist and historian Edward Scobie. The two men had known each other since the 1930s, brought together through a common interest in poetry. Scobie's poems were included in *Poesy Book II* (under his birth name Vivian Dalrymple). He and Casimir continued to correspond while Scobie was in London and resumed their friendship on Scobie's return home in the mid-1960s when he took over the editorship of the *Dominica Herald* from Allfrey. Scobie, who was also involved in local politics, served as vice president of the Dominica Freedom Party, was elected to the Roseau Town Council in 1968 and was its mayor in 1970. Political demonstrations in which Scobie was involved against the government in December 1971 turned ugly and may well have influenced Scobie's move to the US in 1972. There he took up a post as a professor of history in the Black Studies department of City College, New York. Correspondence between them continued in the years following his departure.

Casimir maintained some important friendships internationally, through a common cause in politics or mutual interest in poetry. One such was with Langston Hughes, with whom Casimir corresponded for many years (see also chapter 6). In letters (they never met), they discussed their poetry and Casimir's compilation of the four anthologies of Dominican poetry.

In a letter dated 8 January 1954, Hughes, writing from 20 East 127th Street in New York, says: 'I have just received the copy of POESY: An Anthology of Dominica Verse Book III. It was indeed kind of you to be so thoughtful to send me this collection of poetry. I am happy to have it to add to my collection of West Indian poetry. Thank you, too, for sending me the autographed copies of the poems: *MORE COURAGE YET, TEARS, TITANIA* and *SINCE YOU SAID GOODBYE*. I appreciate very much having them and they also, shall join my West Indian collection as valuable additions. I hope you enjoyed the holidays and you have my best wishes for a happy and prosperous New Year. Sincerely yours, Langston Hughes.'[293]

Again, on 27 September 1958, Hughes writes: 'Very nice to get your note and poem *"Onward"*. Thanks a lot. Here in New York there have been numerous Federation[294] meetings and on Sept 2, (every year) there is a West Indies Day parade. Here is a snap of a part of it I took... No, I didn't go to England. My show didn't last very long there. But I am leaving this coming week for a long lecture tour all the way to California, to be gone for several weeks. Meanwhile my *"Book of Negro Folklore"* will be published in November, also a little novel about gospel churches, *"Tambourines to Glory"*. Cordial Regards to you ever - Langston Hughes.'[295]

Regularly, the two men would send each other Christmas and New Year greetings, exchange photographs and reports of their activities. Hughes' last message to Casimir came in time for Christmas 1966, a few months before Langston's death on 22 May 1967. He wrote: 'Dear Casimir, So good to have your card. I'm recently back from a long poetry Tour of Africa — Coast to Coast — Dakar to Zanzibar. Haile Selassie gave me a medal!... Happy holidays to you. Langston Hughes.' When he heard of Hughes' death, Casimir said that he was heartbroken and wept to hear of his friend's passing.[296]

Closer to home, he maintained a long friendship with Cuthbert Seignoret,[297] who had spent many years as a manager in the oil industry in Curaçao, and his wife Dona. They were generous neighbours and gave Casimir much support after Thelma's death. Seignoret was a great conversationalist, an erudite man full of ideas which they would discuss over a 'Scotch'. Also important to Casimir was his abiding friendship with Louisa Benoit, a well-known seamstress, who kept the art of the *wob dwiyet* alive and passed her skill on to many other seamstresses in Dominica and St Lucia. They found a comfortable companionship in their friendship until the end of his life.

Casimir's last overseas trip was to Jamaica, in 1970. When the remains of Marcus Mosiah Garvey were reinterred in Jamaica in 1964, Casimir had taken a keen interest and had collected the special edition of *The Gleaner* with its double-page spread devoted to this event.[298] Garvey's remains were buried in the King George Memorial Park in Kingston. Later, he was named as Jamaica's first National Hero and the site of his reburial was renamed National Heroes Park. Casimir had long wanted to visit his hero's grave and, taking a rare holiday, he travelled on the *Federal Maple* to Jamaica.

On the way, the boat stopped in Montserrat where Casimir visited an old friend, Sylvia Osborne (née Blanchard) from Dominica. who had married a local businessman Michael Symons Osborne. He also visited the Presbytery to see Rev Fr Joseph Strikers, who had previously served with the Roman Catholic community in Dominica. Another stop was in St Kitts where Casimir met up with James Claxton, an old friend who had been the legal clerk for Sir Clement Malone, chief justice of the Windward and Leeward Islands.[299]

Casimir's visit to Jamaica did not begin well. On arrival he had an unpleasant and humiliating experience. Attempting to pay the 10 cent bus fare, he presented the conductress with an EC$1.00 note. She rudely rejected this and demanded American currency. In the end he was rescued by a sympathetic fellow passenger.

After spending some time at the University of the West Indies campus, he visited Amy Jacques Garvey, Marcus Garvey's widow with whom he had often corresponded.[300] She was expecting him, and, giving him a warm welcome, entertained him at her home where they spent two hours talking about Garvey and topical issues, such as the role of the United Nations.

The following day, he went to the Jamaica Theological Institute to meet with the Jamaican priest Monsignor Gladstone Williams. Casimir was particularly elated by this meeting with the priest who had delivered the homily at Garvey's reinterment, and was said to have influenced the political thinking of both Norman Manley and his son Michael.[301]

On his final day in Jamaica, Casimir visited the Marcus Garvey Mausoleum, 'at which the red, black and green flag was gently waving in the breeze'.[302] He spent some time in reflection and noted the other statues of those who had merited acclaim. Casimir would be satisfied to know that Garvey's fight had not been in vain. There are now memorials recognising the importance of Garvey's contribution and

Garvey and his wife Amy Jacques Garvey.
Casimir met Amy during a visit to Jamaica in 1970.

leadership to the 'emergence and development of black consciousness, black pride, black dignity and black culture'[303] all over the world. Schools, colleges, highways, streets and buildings have been named in his honour.

The 1970s were a time of ferment and change in Dominica and the rest of the Caribbean. Young people who had left the island to study abroad began to return. They had high hopes for the future but had returned to find that unemployment was high and that there were few opportunities for graduates. The only pathways open to them were in the Civil Service or teaching. Such local conditions coincided with the rise of the Black Power movement in North America. It was an attractive rallying call for Dominican youth urging radical change. This did not always meet with general approval and was described by one Dominican academic as being expressed in a number of ways 'be it the shouting of black slogans or self-conscious black rhetoric, Afro hairstyles, cultural patois sayings, walking bare footed, dressing in a dashiki... or being a critic at large of Dominican society.'[304]

However, it is undeniable that this surge in grassroots activism raised the consciousness of many of the youth and had made a serious educational and political impact. There were regular gatherings where young people would meet to fiercely debate history, politics and the issues of the day. This morphed into the formation of the Movement for a New Dominica (MND). The main thrust of the movement was to raise the political consciousness and critical awareness of Dominican youth. At the core of the movement was the belief that the section of the society who held the wealth were in alliance with white foreigners to keep the majority of the population in poverty.[305] Its main objectives were to bring about land reform leading to the redistribution of the land and political transformation to bring more political power to the ordinary people. It was a movement sparked off by school students and supported by returning university students.[306]

This movement was viewed by Patrick John, then the island's premier, as the manifestation of a communist threat.

It was during this period that the Dreads came into existence. Taking their name from Bob Marley's iconic song 'Natty Dread', they were a diverse group: a peaceful element looking to live closer to nature and to reject materialism; political activists; and criminal elements responsible for the murder of some white visitors and residents.[307] In 1974, the Dread Act was passed. This was, in essence, a declaration of war against anyone wearing the distinctive hairstyle associated with their lifestyle. They could be arrested on sight.

Casimir did not find much to admire about the new radicals of the MND. He was firmly in the camp of the DFP, under the leadership of Eugenia Charles, known as the Iron Lady of the Caribbean. In an interview in 1986 with Charles' biographer Janet Higbie,[308] Casimir stated his opposition to the local Black Power movement. He thought that they were rash and had misunderstood Garveyism. He believed that although Garvey had spoken against the white man he did not expect black folk to behave totally negatively against white people. He told Higbie, 'He [Garvey] had many white associates. He wanted to arouse his followers so black people would stop seeing themselves as inferior.'[309] Casimir's poem 'Black Man Listen', written during the Black Power period, emphasises this: 'You oft quote Marcus Garvey, but/ Garvey's philosophy was to educate/ build, unite, uplift/ nothing destructive nor reckless.'[310] He opposed the MND for advocating that property should be taken from the upper classes: 'They burned Nassief's place, thought the government would give the land to them. That was stupid.'[311] His stance was not uncommon among an older generation who were openly critical and scornful of the local Black Power activists.[312]

Dominica gained independence in November 1978 under Patrick John, who became the island's first prime minister, but the following year was turbulent; it was Dominica's 'annus horriblis'. Growing unrest culminated, on 29 May 1979, in a demonstration led by the Civil Service Association (CSA) to protest against proposed new legislation which would restrict the power of the unions. The Dominica Defence Force responded by tear gassing the demonstrators and firing into the crowd. Nine civilians were injured and one young man was killed.

In the face of the government's refusal to accept responsibility for the events of 29 May and its determination to plough ahead with the proposed legislation, a strike was called. 'All trade unions and businesses immediately went on strike and resolved to close the whole island down until the government resigned.'[313] The Committee for National Salvation, drawing its support from the left, moderates, the business sector, the Church, the farmers and the unions was formed and became an interim government for 20 days. During this interval, the Court House and Registry building were set on fire, accompanied by looting and disorder, believed to have been the work of pro-Patrick John supporters. The strike ended on 20 June following the resignation of the now discredited John.[314]

Casimir had responded to these events in poetry. In a poem of encouragement to Eugenia Charles, 'Mama, Keep Going', he dubbed Patrick John as 'Papa Lang Sal'.[315] He castigates members of the opposition and addresses her as 'fearless freedom fighter'.[316]

Later that year, on 29 August, Hurricane David, a category 4 hurricane, devastated the island and its economy. Casimir, Thelma, Rupert and his family who were visiting from Ethiopia, sat it out in the ancient stone kitchen of the Casimir house on Old Street. The house lost its roof and the kitchen remained a refuge for some time.

Dame Eugenia Charles came to power in 1980 and made history as the first female prime minister in the region. In many ways, the conservative Charles, who was admired by the merchant class, found an unlikely ally in Casimir. However, as we have seen, her father, JB

*Casimir supported the Dominica Freedom Party of
Eugenia Charles, prime minister of Dominica 1980-95.*

Charles, had been an early supporter of Casimir and the UNIA, and
in an interview with Irving André in 1997, Charles mentioned that
her father, had been a Pan-Africanist who, for business reasons, kept
his opinions private. 'He was very proud of his race... and believed in
Africa as his home,' she said.[317] Much of Casimir's poetry during this
period confirms his admiration of Charles, and a number of his poems
are praise songs to her comparing her to 'the Maid of Orleans' and
'Queen Nzingha of Matamba'.[318]

Further political turbulence faced Dominica. In 1981, eight Dreads
armed with rifles and machine guns, kidnapped and later murdered
Ted Honychurch, a farmer and village councillor. They burned his
house at Giraudel, a community not far from Roseau, and its contents
to the ground. The house was also the home of Ted's son, the historian
Lennox Honychurch, who at the time was the government's press
secretary. 'Had they planned to destroy a part of Dominica's heritage,
they could not have made a better choice,' Lennox Honychurch wrote,
'for the house was packed with a mass of historical material and

artefacts as well as Mrs Honychurch's copious notes and drawings on the flora and herbal medicines of the Caribbean.'[319] Lennox Honychurch, who lost all his books and possessions in the fire, told me some time later that on hearing of the destruction of his library Casimir had given him a number of books to help him to begin the process of rebuilding his collection. It was a characteristic act of generosity.

Much of the recognition of Casimir's contribution to Garveyism in the Caribbean has come through the work of Professor Robert A Hill of the University of California Los Angeles. The most pre-eminent scholar on Garvey and Garveyism, Hill, a Jamaican by birth, has spent almost 40 years gathering together the papers and history of the UNIA, the largest organised movement of black people in history. Hill is the editor-in-chief of the 15-volume publication, *The Marcus Garvey and the United Negro Improvement Papers*, and it is in the final five volumes identified as the 'Caribbean Series' that Casimir's role in the movement is credited.

Casimir's UNIA affiliations and activities feature prominently in volumes 11, 12 and 13. His importance within the Caribbean Divisions of the organisation is stated in the Historical Commentary of Volume XI (2011): 'Were it not for Ralph Casimir... there would be little historical evidence linking this period of political ferment and change in Dominica with Marcus Garvey and the UNIA. Ralph Casimir's papers show there was a clear, albeit fleeting connection between Dominica and Garveyism.'[320] A group photograph of the Dominica Division of the UNIA is set in the fly leaf of Volume XII (2014) and Casmir is prominently featured in the introduction where it is claimed that he rendered 'outstanding literary and organizational service to the movement not only in Dominica but also throughout the Eastern Caribbean. His work stands out among the documents recorded in the present volume.'[321]

A full-length photograph of him graces the opening pages of Volume XIII (2016). There is also a paean of praise for his organisational skills of the Dominica Divisions, pointing to 'the efficiency and quality of their functioning'. Dominica is cited as 'the strongest outpost in the English-speaking Caribbean' pointing out that Casimir had set up and supervised the functioning of the Trinidad divisions.[322]

One of the scholars working on this project under Professor Hill was Dr Charles Bahmueller. In 1984, he went to Dominica to interview Casimir and to collect from him the original papers — correspondence, legal documents, his own writings and printed matter — relating to his activities and those of the Dominica UNIA Division. The papers relating to his writing deal with social and political issues affecting Dominica, the UNIA and the Pan-African movement across the world during the 1920s and 1930s. There is also a wealth of correspondence with significant figures of the time.

The files which have become known as the *Casimir Papers*, also relate to Casimir's activities as agent of the Black Star Line and the *Negro World*. Among the collection are copies of a number of rare publications. These include *The Black Man: His Antecedents, His Genius, and His Achievements* by William Wells Brown, published in 1863, and *The Brownies' Book* which was the first ever magazine published for African-American children and youths. It is viewed as an important moment in literary history for establishing black children's literature in the United States. The first issue was published in January 1920, with issues published monthly until December 1921. Also included are the register of members of the Dominican UNIA Division, their membership registers and certificates, as well as his own writings, from 1919 to 1982, published and typewritten, and holograph poems written on the backs of letters to save paper. Casimir was careful with his resources and meticulous in the organisation of his papers and we are fortunate that he never threw anything away. He even kept his own drafts and copies of the letters that he wrote to his many and varied correspondents.

Together, Casimir and Bahmueller carefully went over every one of his personal papers and discussed the background of each featured local and international member of the UNIA as well as his correspondents in the US, Africa, Europe and the Caribbean. At one point Casimir agreed to have his singing of UNIA songs recorded.

It was only at the end of Bahmueller's stay in Dominica that he persuaded a reluctant Casimir, who was expecting a visit from Professor Tony Martin later that year, to give up the papers that he had kept carefully filed for more than half a century. Bahmueller recounted: 'When the time came for me to return to UCLA, I broached the subject of taking his papers with me for proper library housing and care. He immediately looked gravely at the stacks of documents and told me that he didn't know that he [Casimir] could do that. This would have more or less wrecked my trip,' said

Casimir with Tony Martin, the Garveyite scholar, on a visit to Dominica in 1984.

Bahmueller. 'We were sitting in his office, and on the desk before me, half hidden by papers, were the first two volumes of UCLA's Garvey Project that I had carried with me as a gift. Pushing away the papers so the two volumes were plainly visible, I said, softly, "We're the Marcus Garvey/UNIA papers." That was all the convincing he required — he shook his head and said "OK".'[323] It must have been difficult for Casimir to relinquish the papers, letters, rare books and photographs which he had kept so carefully for almost 70 years. Surely in persuading him to hand them over Bahmueller must have impressed upon him their historical importance and explained how they would be used.

Casimir's papers were taken to UCLA, but are now in the Schomburg Center for Research in Black Culture in Harlem, New York, where Casimir's name is enshrined as one of the key players in the UNIA movement. The Schomburg is a research library of the New York Public Library and an archive repository for information on people of African descent worldwide. It has, almost from its inception, been an integral part of the Harlem community, and is named after the Afro-Puerto Rican historian Arturo Alfonso Schomburg (1874-1938) who, during his lifetime, amassed a personal collection of 10,000 items relating to black history and the African diaspora. He believed that through historical recovery the New Negro would see himself 'against a reclaimed background' which would lead to 'pride and self respect... and make history yield for him the same values that the treasured past of any people can afford'.[324]

Bauhmueller described Casimir as 'a charming and fascinating octogenarian'. They spent a great deal of time together over two intense weeks and Bahmueller claimed that they formed a strong and affectionate friendship. 'I loved him as a son loves his father. A difference in race meant absolutely nothing.' Bahmueller and Casimir stayed in touch through letters and phone calls. 'We had become father and son; and Mr Casimir never failed to entreat me in his inimical manner to return. He would make his voice into sing-song tones and let me know that 'Dominica... is... calling! Calling me back, calling me home.'[325]

Casimir was gifted the first two volumes of *The Marcus Garvey Papers* and was later informed that his papers, for which he received some financial remuneration, would forever be housed in the Schomberg Center. However, it is unfortunate he did not live to see the publication of the three volumes, which make intimate reference to him and the quality of his work, and document his legacy as an important figure in the spread of Garveyism and the Pan-African movement in the Caribbean. The final two volumes in the Caribbean diaspora series — as yet unpublished — will run from 1923 and focus on Garvey's time in Jamaica.

Casimir had received a brief visit in 1978 from Professor Martin, who made his second visit to Dominica in 1984 some months after Bahmueller's visit, to talk to Casimir as part of his research into Garveyism in the Caribbean. This was published as a chapter 'A Pan-Africanist in Dominica: JR Ralph Casimir and the Garvey Movement 1919-1923' in a collection of essays in *Studies in the African Diaspora*.[326] Casimir and Martin continued their relationship through correspondence long after Martin's departure from the island.

Martin's essay on Casimir was serialised for some weeks in 1991 in the *Dominica Chronicle* but, until then, very few Dominicans had known anything about Casimir's work, which had given 'Dominica a pivotal role in the most successful Pan-Caribbean political movement' up to that time.[327]

Recognition on the island came to Ralph Casimir late in life. It was only in his 84th year that he received a letter from the island's chief cultural officer, Alwin Bully, to say that he had been selected as a recipient of the 1984 Golden Drum Award in recognition of his

The Golden Drum Award was given to Casimir in 1984 in recognition of his contribution to Dominica's literature.

outstanding contribution to Dominican literature. The Golden Drum Award is Dominica's most coveted award for the arts and literature. The citation from the Cultural Division is as follows:

'Whereas it is considered that you, J. RALPH CASIMIR have contributed significantly to the development and appreciation of Dominican literature through the writing and publishing of poetry aesthetic in form and meaningful in content, and whereas through your work you have sought to awaken in your readers a realisation of Caribbean consciousness and dignity and have constantly been helpful in advising on literary matters.

Now therefore, the National Cultural Council presents to you the Golden Drum Award for your outstanding contribution to the Cultural Development of Dominica.'[328]

In 1990, in an address on the subject of national pride on the 12th anniversary of independence, Dame Eugenia identified the types of people who should qualify as national heroes. She cited four categories, three of which related to those whose efforts resulted in the development of Dominican society in various ways over time: 'The indigenous ancestors who had opposed the European invaders; the Maroons and other enslaved Africans who had lost their lives in the struggle for freedom; those latter day heroes of the twentieth century who had fought against the colonial powers for the rights and privileges of their fellow Dominicans; those 'who achieved fame, not necessarily in Dominica, but in other parts of the world, where their accomplishments caused others to take notice of Dominica'.[329] Although he is yet to receive the national and official recognition deserved, there is no doubt that JR Ralph Casimir, who devoted his energy to shining a light upon the ills of his society and to engender in his fellow Dominicans pride in themselves and their identity, fits comfortably into the third group. That same year Casimir was also honoured by the Ethiopian World Federation[330] with a lifetime award for his work during the Garvey movement.

In his last years, Casimir was admired by some of the young poets who would look to him for guidance. One such poet was Harry Sealey who speaks fondly of his visits to see Casimir when he was regaled with the stories of Casimir's youth and political activities. Sealey believed that Casimir enjoyed the company of like-minded youth and the opportunity to talk of his past and discuss the politics of the day. Sealey also helped him to get his manuscript for the pamphlet *Freedom Poems* to the printers. It was Sealey he recruited in 1987 when he set out to repaint his Old Street home in the 'liberation colours'. It was a project that he knew his son Rupert would not support so the plan had to be kept from him.

Sealey recounted the incident. 'It was around African Liberation Week when he had money, he decided to have his house painted in liberation colours, red, green and yellow. Your father might have disapproved but your grandfather was his own man. We painted the house. I got two workers in and myself. What a spectacle. Everyone that pass by during that time had a question. Finally, the job was done, and some would refer to it as Liberation House. He paid the workers and after they left, he bought a bottle of brandy. Mr Casimir and I had a few drinks to celebrate.'[331] Later my father, Rupert, would shake his head at the vibrant display of red, yellow and green. The stubborn old man within was tying his colours to the mast. Defiant to the end. Casimir also gave Sealey a gift of *An African Treasury*, a compilation of articles, stories and poems by African-American writers edited by Langston Hughes, which contained the following inscription: 'For my friend JR Ralph Casimir, sincerely, Langston Hughes.' After his death, the poets of the Writers Guild who included Albert 'Panman' Bellot, Carla Armour, Gerald La Touche, Harry Sealey and others held a poetry night as a tribute to his memory, and read his poems. A group of Rastafarians from the House of Nyabinghi honoured him by attending his funeral.

One of Casimir's final wishes was for his remaining books and papers to be gifted to the Roseau Public Library. The collection was presented by his son Rupert some months after his death on 2 November 1996, in a ceremony held at the library. It was received by Ron Green, the Minister of Education, who welcomed the collection 'as an outstanding resource for researchers' while the chief librarian, Anne Lewis, commented: 'Even in death he continues to contribute and play his role of activist.'[332]

A year before his death, Casimir had agreed to give up his independence and make his home with Rupert and his wife Dorothy, at their home in Goodwill. By now, Casimir was suffering from glaucoma and that curtailed his writing. Approaching the age of 98, his health began to fail but his memory remained strong, and he loved to speak of his political past and role in the UNIA. He would have been proud that his work had been, according to the Dominican journalist Trevor Ducreay, 'fearless in bringing to light the ills of oppressive white rule and the rapaciousness of the growing Negro merchant class'.[333] He would have enjoyed such accolades and would have smiled mischievously, and say with a twinkle in his eye, 'I was a bit of a firebrand when I was young!'

Appendix 1

The following contributed their poems to the four *Poesy* anthologies, compiled and edited by JR Ralph Casimir, and published between 1943 and 1948.

Clayton Alleyne was an Englishman, and the headmaster of St Mary's Academy, Roseau; he also represented Dominica as a cricketer and a footballer. He contributed five poems to *Poesy Two*. His poem 'On Hearing of the Fall of France, June 1940' is a plea to the mother country to 'Fight on, great England, never think to yield'.[334]

McDonald Philip Benjamin had poems published in *Poesy Two*.

John Francis Rupert Casimir, the eldest son of JR Ralph Casimir, served as a statistician with the United Nations for more than 40 years. In one of his five poems, 'Be Real', published in *Poesy Four*, he reminds the reader to admire and cherish the beauty of Dominica which rivals anything in Europe.

> You speak of larks and doves and geese;
> *You boast of English nightingales that sing*
>
> Sweet songs — they say the sweetest in the world
> But you forget we have a feathered creature here
> The humming bird with plumes more gorgeous
> Than Europe's or Australia's greatest boast[335]

Joseph Raphael Ralph Casimir, compiler and editor of the anthologies, had several poems in all four *Poesy* anthologies.

Evens Harrington Eversley Dalrymple was a government official from Tobago. He was also the father of Edward Scobie. His poems appeared in *Poesy Three*.

Vivian Edward George Dalrymple (aka Edward Scobie), see chapter 6, had two poems in *Poesy Two*.

Roy Henry Stephenson Dublin was an English teacher at St Mary's Academy, Roseau, and the secretary of the Vielle Case Village Board. He contributed to *Poesy Three* and *Poesy Four*. Dublin was from Antigua, and received a prestigious award in his homeland for his anthology *Tomorrow's Blossoms*, published in 1934 to mark the centenary of emancipation from slavery. The poem, 'The Labourer', in *Poesy Four* is a departure from his other poems in this anthology, giving a glimpse of the reality of the ordinary Dominican's life.

> And often thus begins man's strife
> Struggling for greater shares in life
> Though tried by thought from morn till night
> The labourer toils with main and might[336]

Philip Telford Georges was Dominica's Island Scholar of 1940. Two poems, 'Dawn, Moonlight Ecstasy' and 'Tropic Midnight', appeared in *Poesy Two* and several poems in *Poesy Three*. He taught at the Dominica Grammar School before going on to study law in Canada.

Philip Griffin, a contemporary and friend of Rupert Casimir, became one of Dominica's leading doctors. Griffin's poem, 'This Isle', is also inspired by Dominica's landscape. It begins: 'This isle, this lump of earth, / For her, nature squanders her best;' and concludes that

> She sleeps, this paradise,
> And calmly waits for what's in store:
> No sighs she'll throw no dice.
> She'll better mankind more and more[337]

J Albert Lawrence, headteacher in the 1940s of the Grand Bay Boys' Government School, president of the Dominica Teachers' Union, and, later, chief education officer, contributed one poem to the anthology *Poesy Four*.

Ianthe Lawton-Browne (née Skerrett) was the daughter of Christopher Martin Skerrett, a teacher from Montserrat. She married an English clergyman and died in Essex, in 1962. Separately, she published three anthologies of poetry, now out of print: *Hatfield Peverel* (1950); *The Living Fountain* (1950) and *The Queen's Carpet* (1951). Lawton-Browne made contributions to both *Poesy Three* and *Poesy Four*. The themes of her poetry are religious and celebrate nature. Her final poem in the last anthology stands out from her other poems:

> Dead, the world weeps,
> The world will ever weep when sons and daughters fall
> Dead and the flowers droop upon thy bier
> To form a pall
> Oh that this bloom so fresh, so fair,
> Spreading the perfume of a precious life[338]

Joseph Austelle James. His poems were included in *Poesy Two*.

Cynthia M LeBlanc contributed to *Poesy Four*. Her poems are mostly romantic and idyllic:

> In a sailboat on a dream-night,
> On a river in a tropic isle,
> In a moment of sweet romance
> Kisses rich and tender all the while
> Hold me, darling in the moonlight,
> On a river in a tropic isle.[339]

'Ode To A Mourner', has a darker tone, where she speaks of grief and of the need for the acceptance of death:

> Let not the night with blackened shroud
> Revive dark mem'ries of the past
> …. Beat not your aching heart against the ground[340]

In the 1970s, she wrote the column *Tales of Ma Titine*, a conversation between a poor Roseau housewife and her friends in a mixture of Kwéyòl and English, in Allfrey's newspaper, the *Sun*.

John Samuel Lewis was a close friend of Casimir and headmaster at St Mary's Academy until 1941. He had several poems in *Poesy Three*. One of these was 'Our Departing Recruits' about those who left Dominica to join the forces in the second world war: 'So to the fray to win yourselves the glory/ That your children may learn the story'.

Ethel J Lockhart contributed 16 poems to *Poesy One* and six poems to *Poesy Two*. She was the granddaughter of ARC Lockhart and wrote to Casimir in gratitude. 'I deeply appreciate your reference to A.R.C.L. and if I say this much you can imagine how much more are the feelings of his grand daughter, one of your contributors.'[341] Her poetry was mainly focused on local issues and her love for her island.[342]

> Dearest land to me thou art,
> On thee I have placed my heart,
> Make me on thee to rely
> In the days which are yet nigh.[343]

Richard Christopher Martin was an Antiguan teacher who worked as an accountant and journalist in Dominica. His poems were included in *Poesy Two*.

Daniel Alexander Nicholas, headteacher of the Clifton Government School, had his work in all four anthologies. His poem 'Dark Shades' explores shame.

> A man who with fantastic tricks
> Would make the angels weep
> Realises in his mighty fix
> That GOD is not asleep[344]

Wilfred OM Pond, headmaster of Hampstead Government School, was one of four contributors to *Poesy One*. Some decades later, he would compose the lyrics of Dominica's National Anthem, 'Isle of Beauty, Isle of Splendour'. He contributed four poems to the anthology.

Christopher Martin Skerrett. His poetry was included in *Poesy Two*. He was a teacher from Montserrat who worked in Dominica for many years. He published *Small Musings*, an anthology of his poetry.

Daniel Thaly (see chapter 6). His poems were published in *Poesy Two*, *Three* and *Four*.

Appendix 2

The J RR Casimir Papers 1919 - 1981

Archived at the Schomburg Center for Research in Black Culture, Manuscripts, Archives and Rare Books Division 515 Malcolm X Boulevard (135th St and Malcolm X Blvd) New York, NY 10037

These papers consist of correspondence, legal documents, and printed matter relating to Casimir's writing. They focus on social and political issues affecting the island of Dominica, the Universal Negro Improvement Association (UNIA), and the Black nationalist movement worldwide, during the 1920s and 1930s. Significant correspondents include: Marcus Garvey, founder of the UNIA; Casely Hayford, *Gold Coast* (Ghana) editor and author of *Ethiopia Unbound*; Malaku Bayen, of the Ethiopian World Federation; Sylvia Pankhurst, editor of the *New Times* and *Ethiopia News*; John E Bruce, African American journalist; Monroe Work, editor of the *Negro Year Book*; Langston Hughes, WEB Du Bois, Roy Wilkins, and other staff of *Crisis* magazine; Thomas LG Oxley, editor of *The Poets' Journal*; Victor L Gray of the *Chicago Bee*; and Cyril V Briggs, founder of the African Blood Brotherhood. The dispute between the UNA, the African Blood Brotherhood, and *The Emancipator* magazine in 1920 are well documented in the correspondence between Cyril V Briggs, Casimir, and Anthony Crawford, president of the Inter-Colonial Steamship and Trading Company of New York. Other correspondence files relate to Casimir's activities as an agent of the Black Star Line and the *Negro World*. Rare publications include *The Black Man, The Brownies' Book, The Challenge, The Comet,* as well as scattered issues of *The Messenger* and a complete run of *The Crusader,* September 1918 to August 1921. Also in the collection are the membership register and certificates of the Dominica Division of the UNIA. Casimir's writings span from 1919 to 1981 and consist of typewritten and published poems, as well as several holograph poems written on the back of letters.

Notes

Chapter 1

1. This category 4 hurricane made landfall in Dominica on 29 August 1979. Strong winds battered the island for six hours. Thirty-seven people were killed and an estimated 5,000 injured. Hurricane David destroyed or damaged 80 per cent of the homes (mostly wood), leaving 75 per cent of the population homeless.
2. A concreted area where produce such as coffee beans is laid on sacking to dry in the sun.
3. She had been married to Percy Olivaccé.
4. JR Ralph Casimir Papers, Schomburg Center for Research in Black Culture, New York Public Library
5. Now in the Roseau Library, Dominica, as part of the JR Ralph Casimir Collection
6. A type of local sausage meat
7. Mythological figures of the Eastern Caribbean
8. Elsa Goveia, 'The U.W.I. and The Teaching of West Indian History', *Caribbean Quarterly* 15, nos. 2/3 (June-September 1969), pp1-5

Chapter 2

9. Kathy MacLean, Karen Mears and Polly Pattullo, *A Caribbean History. Hillsborough: a plantation in Dominica* (London: Papillote Press, 2011), p9
10. Joseph A Boromé, 'How Crown Colony Rule Came to Dominica by 1898', *Caribbean Studies*, Vol 9, no. 3, Institute of Caribbean Studies, UPR Rio Pedros Campus, 1969), p6-67
11. Lennox Honychurch, T*he Dominica Story: A History of the Island* (London and Basingstoke: Macmillan Education 1995), p14
12. Hesketh Bell, Glimpses of *A Governor's Life* (London: Sampson Low: London, 1946), p2
13 Honychurch, p32
14. One such migration was that of the author's maternal great-great-grandparents, Peter and Marie Eleanor Léger, who came to Soufriere in southern Dominica from Martinique in 1880 to escape censure from their families.
15. Bell, p27
16. Morgan Dalphinis, *Caribbean & African Languages: Social History, Language, Literature and Education* (London: Karia Press, 1985), p95
17. Honychurch, p200

18. A comic opera by Arthur Sullivan and WS Gilbert

19. Recollections from Rupert Casimir

20. Letter to JRR Casimir from A.B.C. School of Drawing, London, 1918

21. Detailed report on damage caused by storm on 28 August 1916, with an estimate for repairs, colonial engineer to administrator

22. Joseph A Boromé, 'Origin and Growth of Public Libraries in Dominica', *The Journal of Library History* 5, no. 3 (July 1970), p222

23. Joseph Hilton Steber was the grandson of a German seaman who had settled in Dominica, married a local woman and bought property at Bagatelle.

24. Bookbinding log of JR Ralph Casimir

Chapter 3

25. Honychurch, p157

26. Steven Johns, https://libcom.org/history/british-west-indies-regiment-mutiny-1918 Accessed 19/06/2018

27. ibid

28. Lisa Peatfield, https://www.iwm.org.uk/history/the-story-of-the-british-west-indies-regiment-in-the-first-world-war Accessed 19/06/2018

29. David Olusoga, 'Black soldiers were expendable – then forgettable', Guardian, 11 November 2018

30. No mention is made of how many of the dead were black.

31. Peter Fryer, *Staying Power: The History of Black People in Britain*, (Bath: Pitman Press 1984), pp303-312

32. Gabriel Christian, *The Interwar Years and the Caribbean Soldier in Social Transformation, A Dominican Perspective*, Dominica Academy of Arts, 2015, p9

33. Written for an unnamed newspaper. Personal papers.

34. JR Ralph Casimir, 'Dominica and her Afric Sons', *Negro World*, 4 February 1922

35. Francis Carlton Grell, 'An Interpretation of the Political Life Experience of Dominicans in the Colonial and Post-Colonial Situation', (PhD dissertation, McMaster University, unpublished, 1974), p171

36. 'Representative Government', letter in the *Dominica Guardian*, 9 October 1919, signed The Defensor

37. Honychurch, p159

38. Letter from JRR Casimir to Edward D Smith Green, secretary, Black Star Line, 21 February 1920, in Robert A Hill et al, *The Marcus Garvey and Universal Negro Improvement Association Papers, The Caribbean Diaspora Volume XI 1910-1920* (North Carolina: Duke University Press, 2012), p555

39. Tony Martin, 'A Pan-Africanist in Dominica: J.R. Ralph Casimir and the Garvey Movement, 1919-1923', in *Studies in the African Diaspora A Memorial to James R. Hooker (1929-1976)*, eds. John P Henderson and Harry A Reed, (Massachusetts: The Majority Press, 1989), p127

40. Hill et al, *Volume XI 1910-1920*, 2012, p509

41. WF Elkins, 'Marcus Garvey, The Negro World and the British West Indies 1919-1920', *Science and Society*, 36 (1972), pp63-77

42. Colin Grant, *Negro with a Hat: The Rise and Fall of Marcus Garvey* (London: Vintage

Books, 2008), pp30-32

43. Marcus Garvey, 'The British West Indies in the Mirror of Civilization', *African Times and Orient Review*, October 1913. This is an essay in which Garvey exposed the historic prejudice within the Jamaican Civil Service.

44. Grant, Negro with a Hat, p50

45. Tony Martin, *The Pan-African Connection From Slavery to Garvey and Beyond* (Massachusetts: The Majority Press: 1983), p60

46. Martin, 'A Pan-Africanist in Dominica', p128

47. A written report from JRR Casimir to UNIA headquarters. It outlined the conditions and challenges for the ordinary people of Dominica. Hill et al, *Volume XI, 1910-1920*, pp748-752

48. JR Ralph Casimir Papers, Schomburg Center for Research in Black Culture, New York Public Library

49. Hill et al, V*ol XII*, 2014, p67

50. *Dominica Guardian*, 23 January 1920

51. Land taxes were high and many people across the island defaulted on their payments. Attempts to evict one Pierre Colaire from his property in the Au Vent in La Plaine resulted in opposition from the community. The police shot into the crowd killing four men and injuring two women. The governor, Haynes-Smith, and chief magistrate, Le Hunte, were both present.

52. ARC Lockhart, an elected member of the Legislative Council and journalist, was the eldest son of the Honourable Theodore Francis Lockhart, the police magistrate of Roseau.

53. William Davies was a Dominican politician and estate owner who was elected to the Legislative Council in 1881. He and his wife perished in the 1916 hurricane.

54. Sholto Rawlins Pemberton, also an elected member of the Legislative Council, was a lawyer who followed his father and became puisne judge.

55. *Dominica Guardian*, Anniversary Special issue, April 1923

56. Steber, who described himself at the *Dominica Guardian*'s 30th anniversary as 'A boy born to humble parents and with no one do to for him but a dear mother' also stated that the newspaper 'has been my weapon in fighting the battle of my fellowman against oppression in its different guises'. He was to be later described by Boromé as 'a fearless man with an unbridled pen who was no stranger to libel suits'. He was headhunted by many in the region and the US but he staunchly refused because, he believed, 'My country demands my services.'

57. Hill et al, *Vol XI, 2011*, p525

58. I have found very little mention of the Party of Progress in the documents I have been able to examine. Boromé (1969) contends that once Crown Colony became a fait accompli, Lockhart withdrew from active politics; Davies died in 1916; and both Steber and Lockhart died in 1924. Pemberton went on to become crown attorney and first puisne judge; he died in 1937.

59. Hill et al, *Vol XII*, 2014, p67

60. This was a practice which became more common following the influences of Malcolm X and the Black Power movement.

61. Interview with Rupert Casimir October 2016

62. Martin, *Literary Garveyism: Garvey, Black Arts and the Harlem Renaissance* (Dover, Massachusetts: The Majority Press (1983), p31

63. Martin, 'A Pan-Africanist in Dominica', p130

64. ibid

65. ibid

66. JRR Casimir, 'What Ails Dominica?', *Negro World*, 26 April 1920

67. Hill et al, *Vol XII*, 2014, p.xxxiv

68. The Official Marcus Mosiah Garvey Jr full story
    https://www.youtube.com/watch?v=WBDgu9zRK-s

69. Casimir Papers

70. Martin, 'A Pan-Africanist in Dominica', p138

71. Hill et al, *Vol XI*, 2011, p.cxclx

72. Elkins, p63

73. Martin, 'A Pan-Africanist in Dominica', p134

74. Hill et al, *Vol XII*, 2014. The letter dated 5 August 1920 gives details of the joining fee, weekly subscriptions, the regular meeting place, when meetings are held and the attendees.

75. Cecil EA Rawle to JRR Casimir, 26 August 1920, Casimir Papers

76. JRR Casimir to Louis Gardier, 19 February 1921, Casimir Papers

77. Hill et al, *Vol XII*, 2014, p304

78. Martin, *The Pan-African Connection*, p80

79. In 1921, the *Negro World* reported the establishment of the African Orthodox Church stressing the guiding principle of not identifying with any particular denomination.

80. Hill et al, *Vol XIII*, 2016, pp30-32

81. ibid, p26

82. *Barbados Times*, 17 February 1921

83. *Barbados Times*, 5 March 1921

84. *Barbados Times*, 24 April 1921

85. *Barbados Times*, 7 May 1921

86. ibid

87. Grant, Negro with a Hat, p311

88. ibid, p312

89. Hill et al, *Vol XIII*, 2016, pp62-64

90. ibid, p63

91. ibid, p64

92. ibid, p68

93. ibid, pp109-111

94. ibid, p111

95. ibid, p125

96. ibid, p68

97. ibid, p.xliii

98. ibid, pp184-185

99. ibid, p184

100. By this he is referring to the politics of colourism and asserting an inclusion of all those with an African heritage, no matter their outward appearance.

101. Hill et al, *Vol XIII*, 2016, p185
102. Martin, 'A Pan-Africanist in Dominica', p39
103. Hill et al, *Vol XIII*, 2016, p332
104. ibid, pp333-334
105. Grant, Negro with a Hat, p410
106. Interview with Lennox Honychurch, 3 August 2021
107. Amy Jacques Garvey to JRR Casimir, 6 August 1923, Casimir Papers
108. Martin, *The Pan-African Connection*, p79
109. Martin, 'A Pan-Africanist in Dominica', p141
110. ibid

Chapter 4

111. Celebrations did take place on 1 and 2 August 1920 and were reported in the *Dominica Guardian* of 12 August 1920. However, it must be noted that a very similar report dated 12 August 1921 appears in the *The Marcus Garvey and Universal Negro Improvement Association Papers, The Caribbean Diaspora Volume XIII* 1921-1922. This is an error as JR Ralph Casimir was in Trinidad until the middle of August 1921.
112. First verse of 'From Greenland's Icy Mountains'
113. Marcus Garvey 1921 speech reported in the *Negro World*, March 19 1927
114. The UNIA flag is now referred to as the Pan-African Flag. It is believed that it became the template for flags all over Africa as the various nations gained independence. It is still used as a symbol of black unity. After Michael Brown was killed by white police officers in the US in 2014, protesters wielded the flag at their demonstrations. More recently it has featured at Black Lives Matter protests and rallies.
115. *Dominica Guardian*, 12 August 1920
116. 'Africa Our Home' is frequently mentioned as being sung at UNIA meetings in Dominica. It has also been cited as appearing on the agenda for UNIA celebrations in Harlem, but I have not been able to find the song's lyrics in my re-search.
117. Chorus of UNIA National Anthem
118. Claudrena Harold, T*he Rise and Fall of the Garvey Movement in the Urban South 1918-1942* (New York: Routledge, 2014), p23
119. Before Roseau Cathedral was built, Catholic worship took place in a chapel situated where the St Gerald's Hall now stands. The Cathedral was built by thousands of Dominicans who gave their labour free of charge, doing whatever was necessary to ensure its completion.
120. *Dominica Guardian*, 12 August 1920
121. Honychurch, p123
122. Lennox Honychurch, *In The Forests of Freedom: The Fighting Maroons of Dominica* (London and Trafalgar, Dominica: Papillote Press, 2017), p197
123. ibid, p195
124. Saltfish fritters
125. Black pudding
126. A local vegetable stew made with dasheen leaves

127. Martin, 'A Pan-Africanist in Dominica', p131

128. Hill et al, *Vol XIII*, 2016, p17

129. Peter Léger, the author's maternal great-great-grandfather, was an estate owner on Morne Accouma and the local registrar.

130. *Dominica Guardian*, 4 August 1921. Those named, except for the schoolmaster, were also the main estate owners in Soufriere.

131. Percy Olivaccé was my maternal great-grandfather. He married Marie Lucie Léger, daughter of Peter Léger.

132. *Dominica Guardian*, ibid

133. ibid. There is no record of what the 'needs' might have been. However, many of the inhabitants were poor fisher-folk and estate workers.

134. ibid

135. ibid

Chapter 5

136. Interview with Rupert Casimir, October 2016

137. Martin, 'A Pan-Africanist in Dominica', pp124-144

138. Boromé, 'How Crown Colony Rule Came to Dominica by 1898', p54

139. The Union Club occupied a plot of land with adequate space for gardens and tennis courts. Inside was a billiards room and bar with a large central room where dances were held. White residents on the island patronised the Dominica Club, established by Administrator Hesketh Bell in 1901 as a social hub for the white settlers he was attracting to the island.

140. Interview with Lennox Honychurch, August 21 2021

141. Honychurch, T*he Dominica Story,* p164

142. Jesse Harris Proctor Jr, 'British West Indian Society and Government in Transition 1920-1960', *Special Economic Studies* 2, no. 4 (1962), pp273-304

143. Honychurch, ibid

144. ibid

145. ibid

146. Report of The Closer Union Commission, April 1933

147. Franchise was limited and determined by property ownership and income. In the Windward Islands men and women could qualify equally unlike in Dominica where the franchise had not yet been extended to women.

148. Closer Union Commission, ibid

149. Copy of letter from JRR Casimir to PI Boyd, dated 8 May 1933, in family papers

150. The petition 'On Behalf Of Town Jurors' was addressed to TEP Baynes, acting administrator, 1933. Reproduced in JR Ralph Casimir, *Scriptum Selected Writing of JR Ralph Casimir*, 1991, p68

151. Cousin of Casimir's wife, Thelma

152. Casimir to Boyd, ibid

153. Colin A Hughes, 'Experiments Towards Closer Union in The British West Indies', T*he Journal of Negro History* 43, no. 2 (April 1958), pp85-104

154. *Dominica Tribune*, 10 August 1935, p2

155. Unofficial members of the Legislative Council were both the elected and nominated

members.

156. *Dominica Tribune* editorial, 7 September 1935

157. Unpublished letter to the editor of the *Dominica Tribune*, 'The Truth Shall Always Conquer', dated 9 September 1935. Reproduced in JR Ralph Casimir, *Scriptum*, 1991, p59

158. ibid

159. *Dominica Tribune*, ibid

160. Adam Ewing, 'An Ethiopian Tent: Garveyism and the Roots of Caribbean Labor Radicalism 1930s', *Africology: The Journal of Pan African Studies* 10 no. 9 (2017), p204

161. Cecilia A Green, '"To the Scandal of the Public" Sexual Misconduct and Clashing Patriarchies in 1930s Dominica, British West Indies', *Journal of Caribbean History*, Vol 47, no. 1 (July 2013), p96

162. *Dominica Tribune* articles cited: 'Dropping the Pilot', 9 January 1937; 'Sidelights of Mr Rawle's Non Racial Pronouncement on a Racial Issue', 25 January 1936; 'The Alien Problem', 25 August 1935

163. Hill et al, *Volume XI*, 2011, pp748-52

164. Honychurch, *The Dominica Story*, p123

165. *Dominica Tribune*, 10 August 1935

166. ibid, 2 October 1935

167. Report on the front page of the *Dominica Tribune*, 5 October 1933

168. Casimir Papers

169. ibid

170. Rachel Holmes, *Sylvia Pankhurst Natural Born Rebel* (London: Bloomsbury Publishing, 2020), p682

171. Old name for Ethiopia

172. Green, 'To the Scandal of the Public', p9

173. Personal copy of letter from JRR Casimir to CEA Rawle, 8 January 1937

174. Letter from CEA Rawle to JRR Casimir, 9 January 1937

175. Letter from CEA Rawle to JRR Casimir on the occasion of his marriage

176. Grant, *Negro with a Hat*, p434

177. *Negro Worker* was the newspaper of the International Trade Committee of Negro Workers.

178. *Negro Worker*, December 1936

179. ibid, April 1937

180. ibid

181. Hill et al, *Volume XI*, 2011, p.cxcviii

182. Coronation Hall was on the site of where the New Roseau Market is today. It was a converted warehouse which was a popular dance hall for the general public. The Albert Hall was above the AC Shillingford store on King George V Street and a venue for the upper and middle class. Interview with Lennox Honychurch, 18 September 2021

183. IW André and GJ Christian, *In Search of Eden: Essays on Dominican History* (Brampton, Ontario: Pond Casse Press, 2002), p52

184. Dominica Chronicle, 6 November 1937

185. ibid

186. ibid

187. ibid, 17 November 1937

188. *Dominica Tribune*, 6 November 1937

189. ibid

190. SKNIS press release, 26 February 2020

191. JR Ralph Casimir, an extract from poem 'Marcus Garvey – Dead', 1940

192. Resignation letter to Roseau Town Council, 4 July 1945

193. Jenni Barclay et al, *Historical Trajectories of Disaster Risk in Dominica*, 2019, www.ijdrs.com

194. The French who occupied the island up to this time had developed a relatively diversified agro-export economy dominated by small estates owned by French and free coloured landowners.

195. Cecilia A Green, 'A recalcitrant plantation colony: Dominica,1880-1946', *New West Indian Guide* 73, nos. 3/4 (1999), pp43-71

196. Honychurch, *The Dominica Story*, p185

197. Balahoo Town was a flat swampy extension of the Goodwill sugar estate which became a row of fisherfolk settlements along the shore north of the mouth of the Roseau River. The name was derived from the Kalinago name Balaou, a type of fish caught by the fishermen. When Anglicised, it was pronounced as Balahoo. The area was also known as *l'od bor* in Kwéyòl, from the French *l'autre bord* (the other side of the river).

198. Petition on behalf of the people of Pottersville, 5 March 1947

199. Response from the governor's office, 19 March 1947

200. Letter from JRR Casimir to His Excellency Sir Arthur Francis Grimble, 25 March 1947, reproduced in Scriptum

201. Letter from JRR Casimir to His Honour EP Arrowsmith, 26 July 1947, reproduced in *Scriptum*

202. Dominica official *Gazette*, April 1951

203. ibid, 23 February 1953

204. ibid

205. Dominica official *Gazette*, 29 April 1954

206. Casimir's manifesto for a by-election for the Roseau North constituency

207. *Dominica Chronicle*, 9 March 1955

208. ibid

209. Personal interviews with Clara Casimir (21 February 2021) and Octavia Rogers (22 March 2021)

210. *Dominica Chronicle*, 25 March 1955

211. Frank Baron was the founder of the Dominica United People's Party (DUPP).

Chapter 6

212. Lizabeth Paravasini-Gebert, 'A Forgotten Outpost of Empire: Social Life in Dominica and the Creative Imagination', *Jean Rhys Review* 10, nos. 1-2 (1999), p13

213. R Ralph Casimir, 'My Books', *Negro World*, 11 November 192

214. Letter from Randall H Lockhart to JRR Casimir, dated 25 October 1924

215. ibid

216. JRR Casimir, written for an unnamed newspaper, 24 September 1919. Personal papers
217. Martin, *Literary Garveyism*, p40
218. Marcus Garvey, 'African Fundamentalism', *Marcus Garvey Life and Lessons*, eds. Robert Hill & Barbara Blair (Berkeley: University of California Press, 1987), pp3-25
219. Martin, *Literary Garveyism*, p31
220. *Pater Noster and Other Poems; Africa Arise and Other Poems; Dominica and Other Poems; A Little Kiss and Other Poems; The Negro Speaks; Black Man Listen and Other Poems; Farewell and Other Poems; Freedom Poems; Hurricane and Other Poems; Poesy An Anthology of Dominica Verse Books One, Two, Three, Four*
221. JR Ralph Casimir, 'The Negro World', *Negro World*, 11 November 1921
222. JR Ralph Casimir, 'To the Africans At Home', *Gold Coast Leader*, 1922
223. Martin, ibid
224. Paravasini-Gebert, *Jean Rhys Review*, p18
225. JR Ralph Casimir, 'Dominica and her Afric Sons', *Negro World*, 4 February 1922
226. Reena N Goldthree, 'Writing War and Empire: Poetry, Patriotism, and Public Claims-Making in the British Caribbean', eds, Shalini Puri and Lara Putnam, *Caribbean Military Encounters*, (London: Palgrave, Macmillan, 2017), p62
227. JR Ralph Casimir, 'To Joseph Hilton Steber', *Farewell (And Other Poems)*, 1971
228. JR Ralph Casimir, 'Greetings, Dame Eugenia', in *Freedom Poems*, 1985
229. *Star*, December 1968
230. JR Ralph Casimir, 'Letter', 1973
231. JR Ralph Casimir, 'I Remember (for Dee Jay)', 1972
232. JR Ralph Casimir, 'Two Little Eyes', 1948
233. JR Ralph Casimir, 'You's scarce, me lassie', 1922
234. JR Ralph Casimir, 'Fete Carnaval', 1991. A loose translation of this verse: 'We know carnival time is a joyful time / Everyone come celebrate carnival / Come best friend, let us sing / Come, girlfriend, let us dance.'
235. Flyleaf of JR Ralph Casimir, *Black Man Listen And Other Poems*, 1978
236. Martin, '*A Pan-Africanist in Dominica*', p130
237. Casimir's personal diary, 1921-1924
238. Martin, *Literary Garveyism*, p31
239. JR Ralph Casimir, 'To the Africans At Home', *Poesy An Anthology of Dominica Verse Book One* (Barbados: Advocate Company Ltd, 1943)
240. ibid
241. Lizabeth Paravasini-Gebert (ed), *Love for an Island: The Collected Poems of Phyllis Shand Allfrey* (London and Trafalgar, Dominica: Papillote Press, 2014), p1
242. Daniel Thaly, 'Clair De Lune A Minuit', *Poesy An Anthology of Dominica Verse Book Four*, (ed) JR Ralph Casimir (Barbados: Advocate Company Ltd, 1948). English translation of 'Moonlight at Midnight': Roseau at night seems a city/Of one thousand and one nights/With the scents of the gardens of the island/Mingling with those of the fruits
243. Letter to JR Ralph Casimir from Vivian Dalrymple (aka Edward Scobie), 12 July 1957
244. Letter from Wycliffe S Bennett, secretary of The Poetry League of Jamaica, to JRR

Casimir, 7 September 1950

245. ibid, 16 November 1950

246. Letters from Thomas L G Oxley to JRR Casimir, dated 10 July 1924, 3 November 1924, 18 December 1924, 14 March 1925

247. ibid, 10 July 1924

248. Casimir, *Scriptum*, 1991

249. Casimir, *Dominica Chronicle*, 2 February 1955

250. Casimir, 'Poets And Their Critics', Dominica Chronicle, 2 February 1955

251. Casimir, 'Dominica', 1960

252. Casimir, 'At Peace', 1973

253. Theophilus Albert Marryshow (1887-1958), a Grenadian politician and a key figure in the West Indies Federation

254. Casimir, 'Leader Great And True', *Farewell And Other Poems*, 1971

255. Casimir, 'Farewell Dear Spouse', 1989

256. JR Ralph Casimir, 'Hurricane', first published in the *Star*, 1979, and later included in the anthology *Hurricane & Other Poems*, 1995

257. Casimir, 'A Friend', *Farewell And Other Poems*, 1971

258. Casimir, 'Farewell Dear Spouse', 1989

259. Casimir, 'When I Die', 1978

260. Casimir, (ed), *Poesy An Anthology of Dominica Verse Book Four* (Barbados: Advocate Co Ltd, 1948)

Chapter 7

261. Diary entries of regular communication and correspondence

262. Letter from Maria Casimir JRR Casimir, October 1933

263. It is known that Dudley Casimir had a child, Diego, with Ann Francis in St Joseph. Although separated, he was still married to Maria.

264. Letter from Maria Casimir to JRR Casimir, October 1933

265. Telephone conversation with Enid Elwin who remarked that her grandmother was very strict.

266. Letter from Maria Casimir to JRR Casimir, September 1944

267. Letter from JE Benjamin to JRR Casimir, September 1944

268. Letter from Hubert George to JRR Casimir, October 1944

269. Letter from Hubert George to JRR Casimir, November 1944

270. John Giraud is reputed to have migrated to Brazil in 1908 to find employment which would help the dwindling finances of his family estate. He died in Porto Velho in 1910. In his will, he names his three natural children to whom he leaves 'one house and lot in River Street, Roseau'. John Giraud's parents were John Louis Giraud Senior and Felicité Celaire. He had two brothers Ernest Randolf and George Samuel.

271. The incident is one that has been recounted many times within the author's family, confirmed again by Clara Casimir during an interview, 22 March 2021

272. Cecilia A Green, 'Between Respectability and Self-Respect: Framing Afro-Caribbean Women's Labour History', *Social and Economic Studies*, 55, no. 3 (September, 2006), pp1-31

273. Clement S Jolly, 'Footprints on the Sands of Time', *Tropical Star,* 27 March 1996

274. JR Ralph Casimir, editorial, Dominica Tribune, 26 November 1927

275. JR Ralph Casimir, 'Whither Are We Drifting?' *Dominica Tribune*, 9 July 1931

276. Son of the politician Joseph Fadelle, one of the first black Dominicans to be voted on to the Legislative Council.

277. Irving W André, *Distant Voices*, p24

278. JR Ralph Casimir, 'Christmas Cheer', 1980

279. *The Holy Bible*, Douay version

280. This would be the equivalent of around £67,170 in 2021.

281. Interview with Clara Casimir in 2021

282. Conversations with Octavia (Dolly) Rogers, 22 March 2021

283. JR Ralph Casimir, 'Farewell Dear Spouse', 1989

284. Honychurch, p218

285. JRR Casimir, 'Adieu Mon Cher Ami', *Hurricane & Other Poems*, 1987

286. JRR Casimir, 'Liberation', *Black Man Listen and Other Poems*, 1987

287. JRR Casimir, 'Adieu Capitaine', *Black Man Listen and Other Poems*, 1974

288. Honychurch, *Dominica Story*, p236

289. Transcript of interview with JRR Casimir by Janet Higbie

290. ibid

291. Dedication to JRR Casimir by PS Allfrey in a gifted copy of *Contrasts*

292. JRR Casimir, 'Sweet Home', 1984

293. Letter from Langston Hughes to JR Ralph Casimir, 8 January 1954

294. These were meetings and discussion groups regarding the Federation of the West Indies in 1958.

295. Letter from Langston Hughes to JR Ralph Casimir, 27 September 1958

296. Interview with Charles Bahmueller, April 2021

297. First cousin of Sir Clarence Henry Augustus Seignoret (1919-2002), third President of Dominica

298. Casimir Papers

299. JR Ralph Casimir, *Scriptum*, 1991

300. Casimir Papers

301. 'STGCOBA to Celebrate Monsignor Gladstone Williams', the *Gleaner*, 11 November 2021

302. Casimir, *Scriptum*, 1991

303. Jamaica Observer, 11 November 2021

304. Francis Carlton Grell, 'An Interpretation of the Political Life Experience of Dominicans in the Colonial and Post-Colonial Situation', PhD dissertation, McMaaster University, unpublished, (1974) p279

305. ibid, p282

306. Interview with Bernard Wiltshire who had an organising role within the Movement for a New Dominica, 22 August 2021

307. Irving André, *The War on Dreads in Dominica: From Democracy to Papadocracy*, academia.edu, 2020

308. Janet Higbie, *Eugenia: The Caribbean's Iron Lady* (London and Basingstoke: Macmillan Press, 1993)

309. Transcript of Janet Higbie interview with JR Ralph Casimir [Q: date of interview?]

310. JR Ralph Casimir, *Black Man Listen*, 1972

311. Higbie interview[Q: date of interview?]

312. André and Christian, *In Search Of Eden*, p72

313. Honychurch, *Dominica Story*, p266

314. In 1981, Patrick John, prime minister of Dominica from 1978-79, was arrested for plotting with the Klu Klux Klan and the American Nazi Party to overthrow the governing Dominica Freedom Party. He was convicted and served a five-year prison sentence. He died in 2021.

315. Literally 'Father dirty tongue'; in other words a liar.

316. JR Ralph Casimir, 'Mama, Keep Going', *Freedom Poems* (Dominica: Tropical Printers Ltd, 1985)

317. André and Christian, ibid

318. JR Ralph Casimir, 'Greetings, Dame Eugenia', 1981

319. Honychurch, *Dominica Story*, p278

320. Hill et al, *Vol XI*, 2011, p.cxcviii

321. Hill et al, *Vol XII*, 2014, p.xxxiv

322. Hill et al, *Volume XIII*, 2016, p.xliii

323. Interview with Charles Bahmueller, April 2021

324. Adalaine Holton, 'Decolonizing History: Arthur Schomburg's Afrodiasporic Archive', *Journal of African American History* 2, no.2 (Spring 2007), pp218-238

325. Bahmueller, 'History, politics, and literature on a tropical Caribbean island', unpublished lecture, 1984

326. Martin, *A Pan-Africanist in Dominica*, 1989, p130

327. ibid, p141

328. Letter to JR Ralph Casimir from Alwin Bully, chief cultural officer

329. M Rouse-Jones & Estelle M Appiah, *Returned Exile: Biography of George James Christian of Dominica and the Gold Coast* (Port of Spain: University of the West Indies Press, 2016), p7

330. Set up by Melaku Bayen on behalf of Haile Selassie in 1937, the main objectives of this organisation are: 'We the Black People of the World, in order to effect Unity, Solidarity, Liberty, Freedom and Self-determination, to secure Justice and maintain the Integrity of Ethiopia, which is our divine heritage, do hereby establish and ordain this constitution for The Ethiopian World Federation, Incorporated.'

331. Interview with Harry Sealey, May 29 2013

332. *New Chronicle*, 2 November 1996

333. Trevor Ducreay, 'What Ails Dominica?', *Sun*, 20 September 2000

Appendix

334. Irving W André, *Distant Voices*, 2021, p30

335. F Rupert Casimir, 'Be Real', in JR Ralph Casimir (ed), *Poesy An Anthology of Dominica Verse Book Four*, 1948

336. Roy Dublin, 'The Labourer', in JR Ralph Casimir (ed), *Poesy An Anthology of Dominica Verse Book Four*, 1948

337. Philip N Griffin, 'This Isle', in JR Ralph Casimir (ed), *Poesy An Anthology of Dominica Verse Book Four*, 1948

338. Ianthe Lawton-Browne, 'On The Death Of Miss Florence Mills', in JR Ralph Casimir (ed), *Poesy An Anthology of Dominica Verse Book Four*, 1948

339. Cynthia Leblanc, 'Dew Drops On a Sweet Dream Night', in JR Ralph Casimir (ed), *Poesy An Anthology of Dominica Verse Book Four*, 1948

340. Cynthia Leblanc, 'Ode To A Mourner', in JR Ralph Casimir (ed), *Poesy An Anthology of Dominica Verse Book Four*, 1948

341. Letter from Ethel Lockhart to JR Ralph Casimir, 11 July 1943

342. Irving W André, *Distant Voices*, 2021, p27

343. Ethel J Lockhart, 'Dominica', in JR Ralph Casimir (ed), *Poesy An Anthology of Dominica Verse Book One*, 1943

341. Daniel A Nicholas, 'Dark Shades', in JR Ralph Casimir (ed), *Poesy An Anthology of Dominica Verse Book Four*, 1948

Bibliography

Ahern, Kathleen (2008). 'Drafting a Revolutionary Pushkin: Cyril Briggs and the Creation of a Black International Proletariat.' *South Atlantic Review* 73, no. 2 (Spring 2008).

André, Irving W. *Distant Voices The Genesis Of An Indigenous Literature In Dominica*. Pond Casse Press: Maryland, Ontario, Dominica, 1995. Second edition. Pond Casse Press: Michigan Sheridan Books, 2021.

André, Irving. *Elias Nassief Triumph over Tragedy*. Pont Casse Press: Maryland, Ontario, Dominica, 2012.

André, Irving 'The War on Dreads in Dominica: From Democracy to Papadocracy', 2020. academia.edu https://www.academia.edu/44917135/

André, Irving W, and Christian, Gabriel J. *In Search Of Eden Essays on Dominican History*. Pond Casse Press: Brampton, Ontario, 2002.

Barclay, Jenni et al, 'Historical Trajectories of Disaster Risk in Dominica,' *International Journal of Disaster Risk Science* 10, no 2 (2019): http://www.ijdrs.com/en/article/doi/10.1007/s13753-019-0215-z

Bell, Hesketh. *Glimpses of A Governor's Life*. Sampson Low: London, 1946.

Birge, William S. *In Old Roseau. Reminiscences of Life As I Found It In The Island of Dominica, And Among The Carib Indians*. Isaac H Blanchard Co: New York, 1923.

Blaisdell, Bob (ed). *Selected writing and speeches of Marcus Garvey*. Dover publications, Mineola: New York, 2004.

Boromé, Joseph A. 'How Crown Colony Rule Came to Dominica by 1898,' *Caribbean Studies* 9, no. 3 (1969).

Boromé, Joseph A. 'Origin and Growth of Public Libraries in Dominica,' *The Journal of Library History (1966-1972)* 5, no 3 (July 1970).

Casimir, JR Ralph. *Scriptum Selected Writings of JR Ralph Casimir*. Paramount Printers: Dominica, 1991.

Christian, Gabriel. *The Interwar Years and the Caribbean Soldier in Social*

Transformation. Dominica Academy of Arts, (2009). https://georgetown.academia.edu/GabrielChristian.

Christian, Gabriel. 'Whither August Monday? A reflection on our British heritage, Pan-Africanism and development.' *Dominica Newsonline*, August 2 2020. https://dominicanewsonline.com/news/homepage/homepage-carousel/whither-august-monday-a-reflection-on-our-british-heritage-pan-africanism-development/

Dalphinis, Morgan. *Caribbean & African Languages: Social History, Language, Literature and Education*. Karia Press: London, 1985.

Elkins, WF. 'Marcus Garvey, The Negro World and the British West Indies,' *Science and Society* 36, no. 1 (Spring 1972).

Ewing, Adam. 'An Ethiopian Tent: Garveyism and the Roots of Caribbean Labor Radicalism 1930s,' *Africology: The Journal of Pan African Studies* 10, no. 9 (2017).

Fryer, Peter. *Staying Power The History of Black People in Britain*. Pitman Press: Bath, 1984.

Goldthree, Reena N, 'Writing War and Empire: Poetry, Patriotism, and Public Claims-Making in the British Caribbean,' *Caribbean Military Encounters,* edited by Shalini Puri and Lara Putnam. Palgrave Macmillan: London, 2017.

Goveia, Elsa. 'The U.W.I. and The Teaching of West Indian History,' *Caribbean Quarterly* 15, nos. 2/3 (June-September 1969).

Grant, Colin. *Negro with a Hat: The Rise and Fall of Marcus Garvey*. Vintage Books: London, 2008.

Green, Cecilia A. 'A recalcitrant plantation colony: Dominica, 1880-1946,' *NWIG New West Indian Guide* 73, nos. 3/4 (1999).

Green, Cecilia A. 'Between Respectability and Self-Respect: Framing Afro Caribbean Women's Labour History,' *Social and Economic Studies* 55, no. 3 (September 2006).

Green, Cecilia A. 'To the Scandal of the Public: Sexual Misconduct and Clashing Patriarchies in 1930s Dominica, British West Indies,' *The Journal of Caribbean History* 47, no. 1 (July 2013).

Green, Jeffrey. *Black Edwardians: Black People in Britain 1901-1914*. Routledge: Oxfordshire, 1998.

Grell, Francis Carlton. *An Interpretation of the Political Life Experience of Dominicans in the Colonial and Post-Colonial Situation*, unpublished PhD diss., McMaster University, http://hdl.handle.net/11375/15594 (1974).

Higbie, Janet. *Eugenia: The Caribbean's Iron Lady*. The Macmillan Press: London and Basingstoke, 1993.

Hill, Robert A et al. *The Marcus Garvey and Universal Negro Improvement Association Papers, Vol 1*. University of California Press: Berkeley, 1983.

Hill, Robert A and Bair, Barbara, (eds), *Marcus Garvey Life And Lessons*. University of California Press: Berkeley, 1987.

Hill, Robert A et al. *The Marcus Garvey and Universal Negro Improvement Associa-tion Papers, The Caribbean Diaspora Volume XI 1910-1920* (2011); *Volume XII 1920-1921* (2014), *Volume XIII 1921-1922*. Duke University Press: North Carolina, 2016.

Holmes, Rachel, *Sylvia Pankhurst Natural Born Rebel*. Bloomsbury Publishing: London, 2020.

Holton, Adalaine. 'Decolonizing History: Arthur Schomburg's Afrodiasporic Archive,' *Journal of African American History* 2, no. 2 (Spring 2007).

Honychurch, Lennox. *The Dominica Story A History of the Island*. Macmillan Education: London and Basingstoke, 1995.

Honychurch, Lennox. *In The Forests of Freedom: The Fighting Maroons of Dominica*. Papillote Press, London and Trafalgar, 2017.

Hughes. Colin A. 'Experiments Towards Closer Union in The British West Indies,' T*he Journal of Negro History* 43, no. 2, The University of Chicago Press (April 1958).

Hulme, Peter. 'Islands and Roads,' *Jean Rhys Review* 11, no. 2 (2000).

Johns, Steven. Accessed 19/06/2018 https://libcom.org/history/british-west-indies-regiment-mutiny-1918

Marcus, Harold G. *A History of Ethiopia*. University of California Press, 1994.

Martin, Tony. *The Pan-African Connection From Slavery to Garvey and Beyond*. The Majority Press: Massachusetts, 1983.

Martin, Tony. *Literary Garveyism: Garvey, Black Arts and the Harlem Renaissance*. The Majority Press: Dover, Massachusetts, 1983.

Martin, Tony. *Marcus Garvey, Hero: A First Biography*. The Majority Press: Dover, Massachusetts, 1983.

Martin, Tony. 'A Pan-Africanist in Dominica: JR Ralph Casimir and the Garvey Movement, 1919-1923', *Studies in the African Diaspora A Memorial to James R. Hooker* (1929-1976), edited by John P Henderson and Harry A Reed. The Majority Press: Massachusetts, 1989

Paravasini-Gebert, Lizabeth. 'A Forgotten Outpost of Empire: Social life in Dominica and the Creative Imagination,' *Jean Rhys Review* 10, nos. 1-2 (1999).

Paravisini-Gebert, Lizabeth (ed), *Love for an Island, the Collected Poems of Phyllis Shand Allfrey*. Papillote Press: London and Trafalgar, Dominica, 2014.

Paul, Nalini Caroline. *Identities displaced and misplaced: aspects of postcolonial subjectivity in the novels of Jean Rhys*. PhD diss, Glasgow University, https://theses.gla.ac.uk/474/1/2008PaulPhD.pdf (2008).

Peatfield, Lisa. Accessed 19/06/2018 https://www.iwm.org.uk/history/the-story-of-the-british-west-indies-regiment-in-the-first-world-war

Proctor Jr, Jesse Harris. 'British West Indian Society and Government in Transition 1920-1960,' *Special Economic Studies* 2, no 4 (1962).

Rouse-Jones, M and Appiah, Estelle M. *Returned Exile: Biography of George James Christian of Dominica and the Gold Coast.* The University of the West Indies Press, 2016.

Poetry Collections

Casimir, JR Ralph (ed). *Poesy An Anthology of Dominica Verse Book One.* Advocate Co Ltd: Barbados, 1943.

Casimir, JR Ralph (ed). *Poesy An Anthology of Dominica Verse Book Two.* Advocate Co Ltd: Barbados, 1944.

Casimir, JR Ralph (ed). *Poesy An Anthology of Dominica Verse Book Three.* Advocate Co Ltd: Barbados, 1946.

Casimir, JR Ralph (ed). *Poesy An Anthology of Dominica Verse Book Four.* Advocate Co Ltd: Barbados, 1948.

Casimir, JR Ralph. *Pater Noster And Other Poems.* 60 Old Street, Dominica BWI, 1967.

Casimir, JR Ralph. *Africa Arise And Other Poems.* 60 Old Street, Dominica BWI, 1967.

Casimir, JR Ralph. *A Little Kiss And Other Poems.* 60 Old Street, Dominica BWI, 1968.

Casimir, JR Ralph. *Dominica And Other Poems.* 60 Old Street, Dominica BWI, 1969.

Casimir, JR Ralph. *The Negro Speaks,* 60 Old Street, Dominica BWI, 1969.

Casimir, JR Ralph. *Farewell And Other Poems.* 60 Old Street, Dominica BWI, 1971.

Casimir, JR Ralph. *Black Man, Listen! And Other Poems.* Tropical Printers Ltd: Roseau, Dominica, WI, 1978.

Casimir, JR Ralph. *Freedom Poems,* Tropical Printers Ltd: Roseau, Dominica, WI, 1985.

Casimir, JR Ralph. *Hurricane & Other Poems.* Paramount Printers: Dominica, 1995.

Letters

Secretary of A.B.C. School of Drawing to Casimir, 17 May 1918

Amy Jacques Garvey to Casimir, 6 August 1923

Randall Lockhart to Casimir, 25 October 1924

Thomas LG Oxley to Casimir 10 July 1924; 3 November 1924; 18 December 1924; 14 March 1925

Maria Casimir to Casimir, 5 October 1933

Casimir to Cecil EA Rawle, 8 January 1937

Cecil EA Rawle to Casimir, 9 January 1937

Daniel Nicholas to Casimir, 28 December 1942; 9 May 1944

Ethel J Lockhart to Casimir, 25 January 1943; 11 July 1943; 2 September 1943

Maria Casimir to Casimir, 18 September 1944

Hubert George to Casimir, 2 October 1944

John E Benjamin to Casimir, 26 September 1944

Roy H S Dublin to Casimir, 12 January 1949

Casimir to Johnson Publishing Co. Chicago, 20 June 1949

Harold W Trail to Casimir, 1 September 1949

Wycliffe S Bennett to Casimir, 7 September 1950; 16 November 1950

Vivian Dalrymple to Casimir, 12 July 1957

Langston Hughes to Casimir, 8 January 1954; 29 September 1958; December 1966

Alwin Bully to Casimir, 1 November 1984

Newspapers

Dominica Official Gazette, 22/02/1950; 15/03/1950; 19/07/1950; 01/05/1950; 02/12/1950; 29/12/1950; 02/01/1951; 07/01/1951; 31/03/1951; 02/04/1951; 02/01/1952; 07/01/1952; 22/09/1952; 29/09/1952; 09/12/1952; 23/02/1953; 29/04/1954

Dominica Chronicle, 6 November 1937; 5 March 1955; 9 March 1955

Dominica Guardian, 9 October 1919; 23 January 1920; 12 August 1920; 4 August 1921; 24 April 1923

Dominica New Chronicle, 12 April 1991; 19 April 1991; 26 April 1991; 8 May 1991; 22 March 1996

Dominica Tribune, 7 September 1935; 6 October 1935

Star, 22 December 1968; 20 September 2000

Tropical Star, 20 March 1996; 27 March 1996

Index

Acknowledgements

Writing this biography has been a labour of love. However, it was harder than I thought it would be and took far longer than I ever dreamed! I didn't realise the hurdles that would stand in my way, to name but a few: my husband's cancer treatment, Hurricane Maria, resettling my parents in Dominica, as well as my own inadequacies. Well, I got there in the end but not on my own and have many people to thank for their support along the way; none of it would have been possible without you.

I am indebted to my parents Rupert and Dorothy Casimir and thank them profusely. In particular my father Rupert who fully supported this project. He told me his stories and entrusted me with his father's precious papers, letters and notebooks thus enabling me to have further insight into my grandfather's ideas, beliefs and desires.

I am enormously grateful to my son Ruairidh who read my first drafts and was always so full of enthusiasm and encouragement. His excitement at my revelations, his preparedness to discuss my process and ability to make insightful comments helped me to improve my writing.

Norman MacLean, my husband and life partner, has my deepest gratitude for his unwavering support, encouragement and belief in me. His patience as the project lingered on, for giving me space and doing my share of the housework, being prepared to put off sorting out the attic and all my annoying paraphernalia.

I am thankful to my sons Calum, Tormod and Fearchar for their comments, their interest, their preparedness to have a view and chat about all aspects of the book, especially their opinions on the title and cover. For their pride in me, as well as their humorous approach and ability to keep me grounded.

I am extremely grateful to my sister Karen Casimir Tyers for her unstinting support with research and her help in gaining access to relevant academic articles and photographs. I have also enjoyed sharing our memories and stories, some of which have not made the final cut but would have made the reader smile.

Sincere thanks go to Polly Pattullo, my publisher and editor for publishing this book and really believing that it matters. I am grateful for her encouragement and enthusiasm, for her skilful and sensitive editing and proof reading. Her support with research and tracking down articles in ancient Dominican newspapers. Her patience and preparedness to discuss progress and issues at all stages.

I thank my aunts, Octavia "Dolly" Rogers and Clara Casimir for talking to me about their memories of their father and their childhood. Many thank yous are owed to my cousins Brian Walsh and Penelope Robinson for their support with the process. Thanks to my brother Francis Casimir for discussing his memories of living with our grandparents.

I owe much gratitude to Lennox Honychurch who is a fount of knowledge on Dominica's social history and everything Dominican. He knew my grandfather well and I appreciate how he has generously given me his time and valuable support enabling me to fill the gaps in my memory and knowledge.

I also give my thanks to Harry Sealey for taking time to give me an interview from Trinidad. It was a delight to hear him speak so fondly about my grandfather. I am grateful for his stories which add depth and texture.

Thank you also to Charles Bahmueller who interviewed Grandpa at least three decades ago and carefully took his precious papers to Professor Hill. He spoke so warmly of their time together and was prepared to stay up late at night in North America to speak to me early in the morning in the UK.

I thank Bernard Wiltshire for allowing me to interview him. For his fascinating recounts of the heady days of the 'Dominica Uprising' and improving my understanding of the aspirations and role of the Movement for New Dominica.

Thank you Janet Higbie, who shared the transcript of her interview with my grandfather and for the extremely helpful comments on reading the manuscript.

I am grateful to the staff at the Roseau Public Library in Dominica and at the Schomburg Center for Research in Black Culture in New York for their helpful support; also to Eileen Phillips who worked on the Index and Tania Charles for her sterling proof reading.

I wish to thank all the friends who have made some contribution to my research no matter how small: Jennifer Fadelle Johnson, Ursula Green Johnson, Carol Severin, Dorothy Leevy. I asked questions and you gave me answers or pointed me in their direction.

A big thank you Andy Dark for the careful design of my book and the exquisite cover which prepares the reader so well for its story.

Thank you Chris and Clare Kelly, Marc and Nikki Mellor and Ann and Willy Ross for cheering me on.